Presented To:

_____

From:

_____

Date:

_____

BREAKING
FREE

TOM HAUSER

BREAKING FREE

To LIVE *the* PROMISE
of ABUNDANT LIFE

DESTINY IMAGE® PUBLISHERS, INC.

P.O. Box 310, Shippensburg, PA 17257-0310

"Promoting Inspired Lives."

This book and all other Destiny Image, Revival Press, MercyPlace, Fresh Bread, Destiny Image Fiction, and Treasure House books are available at Christian bookstores and distributors worldwide.

For a U.S. bookstore nearest you, call 1-800-722-6774.

For more information on foreign distributors, call 717-532-3040.

Reach us on the Internet: www.destinyimage.com.

ISBN 13 TP: 978-0-7684-4121-5

ISBN 13 Ebook: 978-0-7684-8840-1

For Worldwide Distribution, Printed in the U.S.A.

1 2 3 4 5 6 7 8 / 16 15 14 13 12

Dedication

To Jack Taylor, Randy Clark, Bill Johnson, Leif Hetland, Heidi and Rolland Baker, and all the other generals who have paved the way and invited us to join them in establishing God's Kingdom on the earth.

Acknowledgments

Thank you, Terry Holler. She helped edit this book and saw the connection of spiritual, physical, and emotional wholeness from a medical perspective.

Thank you to my family and those from Global River Church, who stand with me to help others find freedom.

Endorsement

One of the great privileges in life is to watch God shape His servant according to His pleasure. Tom Hauser is one of those I have watched for years. His life of surrender to Christ has impacted many of us deeply. As a result of His "absolute yes" to God, Tom has been entrusted with unusual insights, depth, and authority in his message on freedom. He is the real deal. Because of his leadership and courage to teach deliverance on trips with Randy Clark, he and his team were given the name Armor Division of Global Awakening. The lessons they learned were obtained in God's favorite classroom—the hellholes of the world, where spiritual warfare is not an option. The stories recorded in *Breaking Free: To Live the Promise of Abundant Life* are authentic demonstrations of God's love and power through vessels willing to learn how to minister like Jesus. I highly recommend both the man and his message.

Bill Johnson, Senior Pastor
Bethel Church, Redding, California
Author of *When Heaven Invades Earth*
and *Face to Face with God*
www.BJM.org

He [Jesus] said to them, "Go into all the world and preach the good news to all creation. Whoever believes and is baptized will be saved, but whoever does not believe will be condemned. And these signs will accompany those who believe: In My name they will drive out demons; they will speak in new tongues; they will pick up snakes with their hands; and when they drink deadly poison, it will not hurt them at all; they will place their hands on sick people, and they will get well" (Mark 16:15-18).

Contents

Foreword by Jack Taylor

A book cannot be separated from its author. For either to be valid, both must be considered in light of the other as equally valid. One could cancel the validity of the other. It's not only the way I judge books, but also the way I try to live my life. To be frank with you, there are some people whose ratings are such that I would be tempted to obtain any book they write. There are others, well…you know!

I don't ever remember using the following two words in one sentence or even the same thought process: credible and incredible, but I found myself using both when I approached the privilege of presenting *Breaking Free* by my colleague and spiritual son, Tom Hauser. I must honestly admit that I am considerably prejudiced in favor of the book, not only because I have examined the book extensively, but also because I know the author. Both are *credible*—they are believable, worthy of trust. But then again, both are *incredible*—seemingly too unusual to be possible. Whichever is examined first lends value to the latter.

Breaking Free is amazing! Let me add some descriptives:

This book is amazingly relevant. While the Church for centuries has generally abandoned the vital ministry accompanying spiritual warfare, namely the deliverance ministry, Tom Hauser and Global River Church in Wilmington, North Carolina, have plunged deeply and effectively into this needed ministry.

This book is solidly biblical. No ministry in which the Church is to be involved demands a stricter adherence to biblical truth than the ministry of deliverance. This book is not just sprinkled with Scripture; it is flooded and soaked in biblical principles.

This book is thoroughly practical. It goes far beyond dreamy-eyed ideas and lands us in the middle of where we think and live our ordinary lives. I have watched the ministry in Africa, with Tom Hauser leading a group in this delicate ministry, not only accomplish the task of setting people free but make other venues of ministry more successful because of the establishment of a culture and atmosphere of freedom.

This book is pleasingly testimonial. Points and principles are driven home by dramatic and graphic testimonies of people finding wholeness and freedom in Christ. Testimonies, of which there are not a few, are tastefully sprinkled throughout that make the reading of this work enjoyable and instructive, as well as just plain exciting.

Finally, this book is impressively inclusive. While the ultimate work of exposing the demonic and dismantling their work is paramount, it would be difficult to imagine this work leaving out equally vital issues like a suggested approach to follow-up and the value of using kind language and maintaining clean breath. I cannot think of anything Tom has not included in this splendid work.

This book is not just a profitable read but serves as a practical guide to the whole spectrum of deliverance. I expect that this fine work, which includes widely accepted models that any church or organization can use, will successfully return the

Church to effective combat. Thanks, Tom, for your willingness to get into the down and dirty to bring people up and clean!

Jack Taylor
Dimensions Ministries
Melbourne, Florida

Foreword by Randy Clark

Tom Hauser's new book, *Breaking Free*, is an exciting and interesting read. Some people might find some of his stories difficult to believe, but he was with me when some of these stories occurred. I vouch for his integrity and honesty in communicating these stories. Tom was initiated into ministry to the demonized while on a team I had taken to Brazil. I still tell of his experience of impartation on almost every trip I take when I pray for the team members. Tom's experience is one of the few stories I tell about pastors who were mightily touched. His experience with the demonic occurred the evening after his impartation.

I have known Tom Hauser for many years and have watched him minister on many of our teams that we have taken to Brazil, Mozambique, and other countries. When I do large crusades, I usually ask Tom to come and head up the deliverance ministry, because he has a strong anointing in this area and is able to bring a large team from his church that he has trained. He has taught deliverance at my Schools of Healing and Impartation.

Tom gives us all hope, because he is not the mystical type; rather, he is analytical. He used to be an executive for General Electric, and he was a nuclear engineer for the U.S. Navy on submarines. He is an unlikely candidate for the ministry of deliverance. Yet, though an unlikely candidate, God has called him and anointed him for deliverance.

I believe your eyes will not only open (metaphorically speaking) to the realm of the enemy in this book, but you will also gain an understanding of how to defeat the strategies of the enemy and have victory in your life.

God has truly anointed Tom Hauser. I am amazed at what God has done through him in the United States, Israel, Nepal, India, Costa Rica, Argentina, Tanzania, and Mozambique.

I believe *Breaking Free* has the potential to become your personal roadmap to freedom, if you need more freedom. It will also instruct you how to bring others into their divine destiny of freedom from the demonic. Regardless of whether your freedom needs to be from direct demonization or from the deceitfulness of doctrines and beliefs that are demonically inspired, *Breaking Free* is your passport to freedom.

It is an honor to write this foreword for *Breaking Free*. Tom Hauser is someone I would always welcome in my foxhole in the midst of spiritual warfare—and be glad he is with me.

Randy Clark
Overseer of the Apostolic Network
of Global Awakening
Author of *There Is More* and
God Can Use Little Ole Me

Preface

You Don't Have to Believe in God to Read This Book

If you are suffering from pain, sickness, heartache, loneliness, torment, or any kind of suffering, I encourage you to read this book. It does not matter if you believe in Jesus, practice another religion, or do not believe in God at all. It does not matter if you have committed the most horrific sins imaginable. The truths in this book provide an alternative to suffering that all people are welcome to discover. You don't even have to be the one suffering; you can read this book to help others.

The only prerequisite to having success with this process is that you open your heart. Be prepared to receive whatever gift the words deliver to your heart.

As you prepare to read, whether you believe in Him or not, ask God to prove to you that He is real. You have nothing to lose by asking this question. If He does not exist, you will simply be left without an answer.

If you believe in God, but have been so dreadfully wounded by life that you no longer believe He is a loving God who cares for you, ask Him to give you a revelation of His love for you.

Now you are ready to *Break Free!*

PART I

An Unlikely Calling

I am going to show you how to obtain God's deliverance from suffering for yourself and others. But first I will answer a question that I am frequently asked: how did a nuclear engineer and executive from General Electric become a pastor who experiences miraculous healings and deliverances?

The simple explanation is that God uses the most unlikely people. The whole explanation requires me to divulge the most intimate details of my life, which I share with you now hoping that my story will help you see the following:

- The miracles that occurred in Jesus' lifetime are not a thing of the past but are occurring in our lifetime as well.

- There is a Kingdom of God as well as a kingdom of darkness.

- We can call upon Jesus to overthrow the power of evil and restore goodness in our lives and the lives of others.

So with this in mind, I now share the experiences of my life with you.

Discovering the Truth

I will send you the Advocate [Counselor]—*the Spirit of truth. He will come to you from the Father* (John 15:26 NLT).

When the Spirit of truth comes, He will guide you in all truth… (John 16:13 NLT).

Then you will know the truth, and the truth will set you free (John 8:32).

My early years are best described as turbulent. My father was a Lieutenant Colonel in the Marine Corps, and he battled alcoholism for many years. The darkness that this brought into our home conflicted with the bright light that shone from my Holy Roller mother, a Spirit-filled Christian who was filled with the presence of God. The great divide between them frequently culminated in household wars that deeply impacted my three younger brothers, one of whom was born with Down's syndrome, and me.

Although I loved and respected my mother, I did not share her faith. As a left-brain intellectual, I required proof of the supernatural things in which she believed. I needed to see it to believe it. I disregarded the spiritual while continuing my intellectual pursuits, which culminated in a Nuclear Science degree from State University of New York (SUNY) Maritime College. I graduated with a Merchant Marine Engineering license and a commission as an Ensign in the U.S. Navy. These achievements further fostered my logical approach to life.

On graduation day at SUNY Maritime College, I married my high school sweetheart, a devout Catholic. We began our life together in upstate New York where I began training as a nuclear power engineer for the Navy with General Electric. My logical brain thrived on the science of operating nuclear, fast-attack submarines.

My work began to awaken my warrior side, as I reminisced about the stories my father and Uncle Jim told of their battles in World War II, Korea, and Vietnam. I absorbed the values of honor, rank, and discipline that these two influential military men and my father-in-law, who fought the Nazis in North Africa, instilled in me. I had become successful in my scientific career and trusted in the logic of science more than an invisible God.

But my life was about to change course. Our 10-month-old daughter, Sara, developed a mysterious intestinal disorder. Food would pass through her undigested, resulting in malnourishment and worrisome weight loss. We took her to numerous doctors, who poked and prodded her, only to report back that they could find no cause.

Eventually the doctor notified my wife and me that there was no medicine or treatment available to help baby Sara—all we could do was "hope for the best." At this moment, I lost all hope. I had no peace. Fear gripped me. If science could not heal my precious baby girl, then where could I possibly turn for hope?

In my fear and confusion, I challenged God and said something like, "I have heard from my mother all my life you're a good, loving God. If you do exist, heal my daughter, and we will talk. If you don't, I will never talk to you again." I look back now and see the honesty of my prayer and the reality of the depth of His love for us.

My wife found her hope through her faith, a faith that I did not share with her. One night she came home from a Catholic small-group meeting and told me that she "got saved." I thought she had gone crazy from the worry that consumed us. My mother had coped with the torment of my father's alcoholism in much the same way, so I considered religion a crutch to deal with life's sufferings. I did not consider their approach to be a logical one.

Nevertheless, my wife persisted. She dragged me to a healing service in Schenectady, New York to hear a former Hell's-Angel-turned-Baptist minister named Reverend Floyd Baker. During the service, I witnessed people being healed and "saved." I thought this was all staged to collect money. But suddenly, the Reverend stopped and pointed directly at my wife and I in the balcony and said, "There is a couple up there praying for a young child to be healed of an intestinal disorder—the child is being healed right now!"

My wife immediately fell to her knees weeping and crying while I pestered her with questions. "Who did you talk to here? Did you talk to an usher? Some other women? Anyone?" Exasperated with me, she replied, "This was the Holy Spirit, Tom. Just believe!"

I was confused. My trust in logic was destroyed. Nothing made any sense to me anymore. Earlier that week, I had become desperate and cried out to God in anger, fear, and rage: "God, if You really exist as my mother and my wife believe, heal my daughter and then we will talk!" Was He really going to heal my daughter as this man, whom I believed to be a charlatan, proclaimed?

When we arrived home after the service, my wife began to treat Sara as if she were well. She ignored the doctors' strict orders and fed her solid food. (I later learned that she was walking in faith, believing in the miracle before it was physically visible.) I held my breath when it was time to change her diaper, hoping for good results. The diaper had good results! From that moment on, Sara began to digest her food and gain weight. Our doctor was surprised and told us to "keep doing whatever you are doing."

When I realized my daughter was healed, I knew it was time to have a heart-to-heart with God. After all, I promised Him that we would talk if He healed Sara. This is what I said, "So You exist. I think your method of communication with me stinks. But You have my attention. My logic doesn't work. OK. Tell me what I need to do."

A few days later, my wife—who was cooperating with the Holy Spirit—set me up. She invited Bill, a former-wine-distributor-turned-Baptist minister, to the house. Bill proceeded to explain to me what it means to be "saved." He told me that salvation—not having to go to hell after you die—is a gift. It cannot be earned by doing good works. He told me that I needed to confess with my mouth and believe in my heart that Jesus is Lord. (I now know this is from Romans 10:9-10.)

At this point I was done with logic. I gave up running from God. I surrendered and prayed to receive Jesus. For the first time in my life I believed that a Savior existed for me. As I sat on the couch praying with Bill and my wife, Ginny, I began to speak in an unknown foreign language—tongues. This is the moment when I left the world of logic and entered God's Kingdom here on earth, which is full of the supernatural.

The thief does not come except to steal, and to kill, and to destroy. I have come that they may have life, and that they may have it more abundantly (John 10:10 NKJV).

As I look back upon my life, I realize that God had to hit me over the head with a two-by-four to get my attention, because He knew I would be a tough nut to crack. Of course, He was right. Although I don't believe that God was responsible for making our baby sick, He allowed the devil to implement a plan to destroy us. God, in His goodness, allowed this fiery trial to pave a pathway to eternal life for me and for many who would follow after me. True to His nature, God turned the devil's evil plan to rob, kill, and destroy into an abundant life.

What a Father to have! What a Savior! Look at the lengths He will go to bestow His love upon us.

CHAPTER 2

A Change of Heart

"And I am certain that God, who began the good work within you, will continue His work until it is finished" (Philippians 1:6 NLT).

I would love to tell you that Sara's healing instantly transformed me from sinner to saint, but that is not the truth. Instead, I would plow forward only to backslide repeatedly. There was even a time when my self-centeredness threatened my marriage.

But God steadfastly worked within me to change my heart. If not for His grace, the tough loving spirit of my wife, and the biblical truth about marriage that a pastor at Grace Church delivered to me, my marriage would not have endured. But it did. Thank you, Jesus! Today our marriage is such a gift, and I thank the Lord for His faithfulness.

God spent many years working on my heart. He used life circumstances to chip away my selfish human nature and to fill me with patience, love, joy, and faith.

In the early 1990s, I was working for Knolls Atomic Power Lab (KAPL). General Electric (GE) held a Department of Energy contract to run KAPL in order to design and operate naval nuclear reactors (submarines and surface ships).

One day, the chief executive officer of GE called KAPL requesting that someone with quality assurance and radiological expertise fly to Wilmington, North Carolina to audit their nuclear fuel plant located there. I was selected. I flew to Wilmington, completed the report, and then returned to New York thinking that I was finished with North Carolina.

But God was keeping an eye on my family, and He had a different plan. He spoke to my mother while I was in Wilmington and told her that we would live in North Carolina. My mother shared this information with my wife. Rather than telling me, she wrote it on an index card and placed it in my Bible where it became lost in the shuffle of many other papers and notes.

One year later, I was offered a position with GE as the environmental health and safety manager in Wilmington. I promptly refused. However, the company persisted, and my wife and I flew to Wilmington to explore the possibility of relocating to the South after 40 years of life in the North. When we returned to New York, I sensed that God was telling me to go, but the fear of the unknown caused me to resist.

My wife and I decided to pray over the decision. As I opened my Bible, many papers fell to the floor. I picked up one of them and read, "Tom in Wilmington, NC 1991, from mom saying, 'you will one day live in NC.'" Needless to say, I took the job.

Eleven days later, GE announced the end of its Department of Energy contract with the federal government after 40 years. Since I had just accepted a new position, I was able to keep my GE pension and an executive position. Many people at KAPL accused me of having prior knowledge of the contractual termination. It was only the grace of God that preserved my career, as others were left without GE benefits or a GE pension. My faith was definitely growing. On December 31, 1992, we packed up our family and moved to Wilmington, North Carolina.

Katie's Influence

God had used our daughter Sara to speak the truth into my heart, and now He was about to use our other daughter, Katie, for several purposes. God has a special place in His heart for Katie, who clearly has no spiritual handicaps despite the physical and mental challenges she was born with. Katie's trials had frequently caused me to question God's goodness, but once again God had a plan to change my heart.

When Katie was about 19, she and I attended a gathering together. Toward the end, she lined up all of the youth and prophesied over them. One by one, God's spirit spoke through her, touching deep places in each of their hearts. While I watched in awe, God spoke to my heart and said, "My ways are not your ways; My ways are higher." At that moment, I let go of the brokenness I had felt as Katie's father and surrendered my heart completely to my Father in Heaven.

Next, God used Katie to move my family from the Baptist church we attended in Wilmington to the Vineyard Church, which was Spirit-filled. We had attended the Baptist church for about a year when we received an anonymous note one Sunday that said, "Keep your daughter quiet during the service." The note was in response to Katie's frequent outbursts of "Amen" whenever her spirit moved her to respond to the sermon. After that, Ginny and the kids left to explore the Vineyard Church; I continued to teach Sunday school at the Baptist church.

A month later, I entered the Vineyard church for the first time wearing my traditional church attire: a 3-piece suit and tie. I was shocked when I saw a man at the front of the church who looked like a biker with a long ponytail and who was wearing a T-shirt that said, "God Rules." Next, my eyes were drawn to the people who were waving flags and dancing around the sanctuary. I was taken aback. My wife just looked at me and said, "Tom, sit down. You'll be OK." Once I recovered, I felt the presence of the Holy Spirit. That was enough for me. I gave up my suit and settled into my new church home. I did not know it at the time, but one day I would come to pastor this church, which would later be re-named Global River Church.

Katie also provided a glimpse of a less traditional form of worship to the Episcopal couple, Terry and Jan Rickey, who previously lived across the street from us. Terry's father and two brothers were Nazarene pastors and he and his wife continued to embrace a traditional relationship with God. But Katie planted a seed in their hearts that led to a radical change in them while they were on a mission trip to Brazil, as I will explain later. Katie planted this seed in a most unusual manner.

You see, Katie receives calls from people asking her to pray for them because they acknowledge her gift of intercession—praying for the needs of others. Every day Katie would sit on the front porch swing of our home for hours at a time, singing her heart out and crying out to Jesus for the needs of people all over the world. Initially, Katie's behavior seemed unusual to our new neighbors; but God moved in them, and they became filled with the same

Spirit that fuels Katie's passion for prayer and worship. Terry is currently the pastor of Discipleship at Global River Church.

Answered Prayers

During the 1990s, there was a marked downturn in the nuclear industry, and by 1997 I was emotionally drained from having to lay off good people. I began to pray for God to move me. One day, while sitting in a meeting with the vice president of Nuclear Fuel, an announcement was made that more layoffs were required. I quietly prayed to myself, "Lord, please move me. I can't do this again!"

Within five minutes, my pager sounded. It was a call from Jack Sependa, a friend who was an executive for the CEO of GE Motor's Division in Fort Wayne, Indiana. I immediately returned the call and learned that God had already answered my prayer. It turned out that Jack was in a meeting at the same time I was praying. The CEO of GE Motor's Division asked the staff he had assembled if anyone knew someone with nuclear or training experience. Jack's hand shot up, he gave my name, and he arranged an interview for me without even hesitating to ask me first.

As I prepared for my interview in Indiana, my wife made one request: to remain in the South. She said she liked Georgia, not Fort Wayne. And then added, "Fort Wayne is not the end of the world, but you can see it from there."

I accepted the job and was pleasantly surprised when the CEO, Jim Rogers, said he wanted us to move to Atlanta, Georgia. (I later learned that all of GE Motors' executive staff moved to the outskirts of Atlanta.) My wife and I smiled at another answered prayer, asked God to show us where to live, and then laid our hands upon the map. Lawrenceville was the town God pointed us to, and so we began the next chapter of our lives there.

Soon after arriving in Lawrenceville, we joined the Gwinnett Vineyard Church, and I enrolled in the Baptist Seminary at Luther Rice University. Our pastor, Scott Westbrook, asked me to be his associate pastor, but I thought, "I'm a GE 'lifer,' not a pastor!" Pastor Scott said he "knew in his spirit" from the first time I had entered the church that I was to be a pastor. I told him that he was wrong. He had to be. After all, hadn't I prayed for 25 years to be promoted to an executive level position so I could work directly with the CEO's team? Hadn't God finally answered my prayers? My heart was conflicted; and, therefore, I was unable to rejoice in my latest career victory. Could Pastor Scott be right? Was I really supposed to be a pastor?

As I continued working in my "dream" job, God began to transform my heart. GE had sold a nuclear reactor to Japan, so I was on a business trip to Hong Kong enjoying the perks of $400 hotel rooms and a lavish expense account. One day, I nonchalantly stepped over a homeless man and heard, "Watch out, rich man!" I believe God put these words in my heart to remind me of the story of Lazarus (his story follows) and, therefore, to encourage me to forgo the perks of an executive lifestyle in favor of a modest life as His servant.

The Rich Man and Lazarus

There was a rich man who was dressed in purple and fine linen and lived in luxury every day. At his gate was laid a beggar named Lazarus, covered with sores and longing to eat what fell from the rich man's table. Even the dogs came and licked his sores.

The time came when the beggar died and the angels carried him to Abraham's side. The rich man also died and was buried. In hell, where he was in torment, he looked up and saw Abraham far away, with Lazarus by his side. So he called to him. "Father Abraham, have pity on me and send Lazarus to dip the tip of his finger in water and cool my tongue, because I am in agony in this fire."

But Abraham replied, "Son, remember that in your lifetime you received your good things, while Lazarus received bad things, but now he is comforted here and you are in agony. And besides all this, between us and you, a great chasm has been fixed, so that those who want to go from here to you cannot, nor can anyone cross over from there to us" (Luke 16:19-26).

On another journey overseas to Taiwan, I was seated next to a Japanese man who, upon noticing that I was reading a Bible passage, commented, "You Christians intrigue me." I asked him why and he proceeded to tell me about his past. He had been a Kamikaze pilot for the Japanese military in World War II. Just before he was scheduled to depart on his death flight, with orders to crash his plane into a U.S. ship, the war suddenly ended when the U.S. bombed Hiroshima and Nagasaki.

The Japanese man recalled that the U.S. servicemen still stationed in his country proceeded to feed his destitute people day after day until they were back on their feet. He added, "You know, if the outcome of the war had been different, we certainly would not have treated your people the same way. Yes, you Christians intrigue me." The Spirit moved within me, and I felt compelled to share the message of God's love with him.

Although I was clinging to my worldly career, I was already functioning as a pastor.

God's next move came in a vision that I had while my wife and I were vacationing with our family in Wilmington, North

Carolina. I saw myself standing next to my senior pastor from the Vineyard Church in Wilmington. Standing with us was a tall man I did not yet know. (He turned out to be a worship leader who would come to lead worship at the Vineyard Church in Wilmington two years later.) Next, I saw two pastors resigning from the Vineyard. One of these men was known to be leaving, but not the other

When I informed the pastor about my vision, he said that nobody knew these details. I said, "The Holy Spirit knew!" My senior pastor said that I needed to pray about joining him as the associate pastor of the Vineyard because too many unexplained circumstances were aligning themselves. He said something like, "This might be the work of 'Jehovah [God] Sneaky.'"

Wow! Now I was scared, because I knew in my heart that God was calling me to this position. But I would make a mere 20 percent of my GE salary as a pastor. I would also lose my stock options and many other perks that I had worked and prayed for. I was struggling with such a life-changing decision, so I decided to cut a deal with God. I said, "God, if You are calling me to full-time ministry, I need to see three things: have my wife be willing to be a pastor's wife and send two people, who know nothing about my situation, to prophetically confirm this calling. Then, I will resign from GE and serve You until I die."

I felt relatively safe with this bargain, because my wife had already said many times that she would never be a pastor's wife. She had seen how difficult and hurtful that could be. (Sheep bites really sting!)

After making this deal with God, I informed my wife that I believed I was being called into full-time ministry. She reacted very negatively and declared that I was having a mid-life crisis. After this conversation, I felt certain that would be the end of the matter.

But the next morning my wife walked into the kitchen and said, "OK, Tom, we can do this." I was floored. I asked her how, in less than 24 hours, she could change her mind so dramatically. She replied simply, "God changed my heart." She had received a dream the previous night. In her dream, God asked her, "Ginny, why won't you trust Me?" Next, she saw herself surrounded by beautiful, dark-skinned, smiling children. Could this be related to a similar vision she had nine years earlier? If so, it suggested that a major life change loomed on the horizon.

When Ginny had the first vision, I remember thinking that there was no way I was going on a mission to Africa! (The fulfillment of this vision began on our first mission trip to Mozambique, Africa, with Randy Clark, Heidi and Rolland Baker, Papa Supressa, and Tom Jones in 2001. About 200 children met our Land Rover in the bush, singing to greet us, and Ginny and I cried about how God maps out our lives if we will only listen and say yes!) The Lord guides us down the best pathway for our lives.

I will instruct you and teach you in the way you should go; I will counsel you and watch over you (Psalm 32:8).

Well, my wife was willing to be a pastor's wife, but I still needed two people to speak prophetically into my life before I was willing to jump ship from a perfectly good career. Later that night, we went to a dinner party hosted by a member of the Vineyard Church, Jane Smith. As she served me a piece of ham, she stopped suddenly, looked me in the eye, and proclaimed, "You need to come be one of our pastors here at the Vineyard. You need to come." Out of the corner of my eye, I noticed my wife was choking on her food. We had just heard the first prophetic word that would confirm a major change in our lives.

We packed our bags and headed back to Georgia. After enduring an eight-hour drive with the kids, we received a call from our friends, Jack and Barbara Sependa. They had once lived in Wilmington and were eager to hear all about our trip. It was out of character for Barbara to be so forceful, but she really wanted to see us that night. Although I was exhausted, I relented and they walked past the suitcases piled in the hall to sit on our deck and talk.

Jack was speaking about something when he suddenly stopped mid-sentence and began to speak in tongues. He then interpreted the tongues and said, "I see a GE symbol with a red line through it. You will not work for GE anymore. You will pastor a large church and your wife, Ginny, and your daughter Katie will be involved in the ministry." My wife looked at me, and we both knew my life with GE was over.

CHAPTER 3

Hungry for More

Then you will know the truth, and the truth will set you free (John 8:32).

I began my new career as associate pastor of the Vineyard Community Church in Wilmington, North Carolina in 1998. By early 2000, I was spiritually hungering for more. I had witnessed Sara's healing years ago. I had studied the Book of Acts and John's Gospel, and I knew that God intended for all of His followers to do the same works, and even greater works, than Jesus and His apostles did (see John 14). The problem? I did not know how to utilize the power of the Holy Spirit.

I had heard about the miraculous healings and wonders involving Randy Clark and the Toronto Blessing.[1] The founder of the Vineyard Churches, John Wimber, taught that every believer should "do the stuff" that Jesus did (see Mark 16:15-18; John 14:12). I did no "stuff," and I experienced little spiritual power. I decided I would go to a Voice of the Apostles conference, because Randy Clark would be there, and I thought I might perhaps find a way to reach this next level of spiritual growth.

While at the conference, I met Heidi Baker, a missionary who has seen numerous miracles, deliverances, and salvations in the bush, cities, and dumps of Mozambique, Africa. As she preached, she explained that the Holy Spirit had "wrecked her." She prayed, "God, kill them until they are good for nothing but You." This was a little too weird for me. Although I desperately wanted more spiritually, I couldn't bring myself to go up to the altar when she summoned, "Everyone who wants to die for Jesus."

But Heidi's message struck a cord within my heart. I knew the Bible instructed believers to give up their lives in order to be worthy of the Kingdom of God.

Anyone who does not take his cross and follow Me is not worthy of Me. Whoever finds his life will lose it, and whoever loses his life for My sake will find it (Matthew 10:38-39).

After two days, I had become so convicted by Heidi's message and the Scripture in Matthew 10 that I decided to give up my life and I sold myself out completely to God. At that moment, Jesus truly became the Lord of my life.

That same day, Randy Clark prophesied that I would be "sent like Paul and Barnabas to the nations." I fell to the ground under the power of the Holy Spirit; and when I got up, I knew I was headed to the nations.

ENDNOTE

1. The Toronto Blessing was a major revival that began when Randy Clark spoke at a small church beside the Toronto Airport. There were numerous healings and manifestations of the Holy Spirit. Millions came to the Toronto Blessing from all over the world to be refreshed and ignited for the Kingdom.

CHAPTER 4

The Mission Field: Brazil

But solid food is for the mature, who by constant use have trained themselves to distinguish good from evil (Hebrews 5:14).

The mission field is the place where I have encountered God's greatest manifestations of power, presence, mercy, and glory. It is also here that I first encountered the existence of a sinister presence from the kingdom of darkness.

Brazil, April 2001

As I packed my bags for my first mission trip, I prayed, "Lord, I want to see Your power." (I later learned to be careful what you pray for!) Eleven members of our local Vineyard church, including Ginny and our daughter Katie, accompanied me. We were all novices. Randy Clark, founder of Global Awakening, and Tom Rutollo, who would later become vice president of International Mission for Global Awakening, both joined us.

Prior to ministering to the people of Sao Paulo, Randy wanted to pray for all of us. We gathered on the seventeenth floor of a hotel in Sao Paulo for "impartation," which involves the laying on of hands to impart ministry giftings (see Heb. 6:1-2).

One member of our team, Tony, arrived late, so I asked Randy to pray for him. We all gathered around Tony and laid our hands on him as Randy prayed.

Suddenly, I strongly felt God's presence all over my body. I fell down and collided with a table and then began spinning on the floor. A nurse who was with us thought I was having a grand mal seizure, but I felt the presence of God's power. Afterward, I noticed that the force of my leg had bent a metal chair and my "unbreakable," titanium-rimmed glasses were bent and the lenses had dislodged. I stood up, felt "out of it," and said to my wife, "Honey, take me home. I'm drunk!"

After this incident, I felt discouraged because I had broken glasses, poor vision, no power, and the memory of my "undignified" display. I would soon discover, though, that God was simply honoring my request to see His power.

Later that night we arrived at Aqua Viva (Living Water), the church we would minister to, and our team was moved to tears as we experienced passionate Brazilian worship. I could actually feel the presence of the Holy Spirit just as I had during my "seizure" earlier that day. I believe I received a word of knowledge from the Holy Spirit (see 1 Cor. 12:8) and told Randy we were to pray for the terminally ill.

Randy invited all who were terminally ill to go to the back room of the church so that our team could pray for them. Twenty-five very sick and dying people surrounded us. They were counting on us to summon a miracle from God.

As the only pastor in the room, I was overwhelmed by the burden of responsibility I felt that was coupled with my lack of experience, power, and ability. I couldn't even see well without my glasses! So we did the only thing we knew how to do. We simply placed the burden in God's hands and began to pray. I was praying for a woman with AIDS, while my wife was praying for a woman named Priscilla.

Our First Deliverance

My wife approached Priscilla, who arrived on crutches, and began to pray for her. She had a sad story to share. When she was one year old, a "Macumba witch" had cursed her because her father had made fun of a child who was crippled.

Born healthy, Priscilla's hips and legs then developed severe deformities that resulted in eight surgeries. They failed to correct a 90-degree curvature in her right foot that caused excruciating pain and misalignment in her spine.

Upon hearing this sad story, my wife realized Priscilla would require deliverance. Deliverance is a means to achieve total freedom physically, emotionally, and spiritually through prayer. The art of deliverance is discussed in subsequent sections.

My wife told Priscilla that I was her husband, a pastor, and would assist in the prayer for her deliverance. I had never before performed deliverance, but Ginny and I began to walk through the steps that we had learned. We began by asking Priscilla if she would be willing to forgive everybody who had ever hurt her, including her father and the school children who rejected her. We then asked her to confess her sins. At this point, I remembered that Jesus had said He had given us authority over all the enemy's power in His name (see Luke 10:19). So I spent the next two hours praying in Jesus' name against spirits of witchcraft, infirmity, pain, rejection, and the like.

During this time, we witnessed writhing movements and sounds that rivaled some of Hollywood's popular exorcist movies. We believe these were manifestations of demons being forced to leave her body against their will. To us, the kingdom of darkness was obviously bowing down in response to the authority of Jesus' name.

After I had cast out every evil spirit I could possibly think of, Priscilla looked at my wife and me and said, "I want to walk." We supported her by her arms as she walked across the room. As her faith increased, her legs, hip, and back began to straighten. Everyone in that room began to celebrate and praise Jesus. We all saw His power! I was humbled by the thought that He would use little old me to do "the stuff." It was beyond words.

When Priscilla's husband walked into the room with their 1-year-old son, we all rejoiced together. We went crazy for Jesus all over again. It was a very emotional night; but when everyone settled down, I noticed that her right foot was not 100 percent straight. It deviated to the right, not by an excruciating 90 degrees like it had when she arrived, but by about 10 degrees. Priscilla and her family were ecstatic over the results and didn't question the minor imperfection. But, as a detail-oriented former nuclear engineer, this didn't sit right with me. I asked, "Lord, why didn't You do it all the way? Why did You heal and deliver her, yet leave this slight imperfection?"

As I retired for the evening, I began to process all the miracles that had occurred that night. The deaf heard, tumors disappeared, the lame walked, and the demonized were set free. The warrior side of me was being awakened. I knew God would anoint me for more deliverances; I was on fire with purpose and destiny.

The next night we arrived at Aqua Viva church to find an even larger crowd than the night before. I scanned the crowd in search of Priscilla and located her worshiping with her husband and son. I began praying for her, "Lord, just get her all. God, touch her." Then I noticed that she started shaking, as if she were hanging on to an electrical wire. I pushed forward through the crowd until I reached her. Her husband looked at me with eyes that pleaded, "What now?"

I felt the Holy Spirit rise within me. And although I knew very little Portuguese, I confidently declared to the still-shaking Priscilla, "Seja curado em nome de Jesus!" ("Be healed in the name of Jesus"). Immediately her foot moved. It became completely straight, and she stood up totally healed. God had fully answered my prayer request, and I had seen His power just like in the Book of Acts. We worshiped with such abandon!

On that first trip to Brazil, we visited several other churches and saw nearly 2,000 healings and 400 salvations. Our team was blessed to witness such an incredible outpouring of the Holy Spirit. We returned to Wilmington to share our experiences and demonstrations of the power of the Kingdom of God.

September 11, 2001

Our team's incredible testimonies sparked great interest in missions and a new team was assembled to return to Brazil. We were advised to keep a low profile because the miracles, signs, and wonders were being noticed, and we didn't want any trouble obtaining future travel visas.

On the morning of September 11, 2001, some of our team members arrived at Rio de Janeiro on the first flight from the U.S. that morning. When we heard the horrific news about the World Trade Center attacks, we gathered in a coffee shop around the only television airing CNN. We watched in horror while wondering how many other planes the terrorists may have hijacked. We still had some of our team members in the air.

Our worship team broke out their instruments and began to worship together. One worship leader had borrowed a guitar that had an "I love New York" sticker on the case. When the Brazilian press heard that there were New Yorkers in Rio who were awaiting others from the U.S., we ended up on television. So much for the low profile we had been advised to keep!

As each plane arrived, our worship music was audible all the way through customs, moving many international travelers to join us. The airport janitors danced with their brooms. A Korean Christian sang, "These Are the Days of Elijah" for us in Korean. Randy Clark was the last to arrive, and we rejoiced at the safe arrival of our entire team.

The events of 9/11 meant that we would not be able to travel home for an extended time. But we were in Brazil to lift up Jesus, and that is what we intended to do for as long as we were there. On this trip, we witnessed an exponential increase in healings and miracles. I inquired of the Lord about why we witnessed so many overt miracles in Brazil, while the Holy Spirit's movements were less obvious in the U.S.

I received my answer at a church in Manuas. It was a poor but powerful church with 46,000 parishioners. The church had a roof, but no sides. When we arrived, the Brazilian church dance team performed a tribute to America to the tune of "Amazing Grace." The dancer who was closest to me was draped in the American flag in tribute and had wept a puddle—I am not exaggerating—for

Jesus to save America with His amazing grace. I weep even now as I recall it years later.

The Holy Spirit spoke to my spirit at that moment saying, "Tom, if you wonder why I come to Brazil with power, it is because of their passion for Me." I knew in my heart that this was truth, so I prayed for America to return to our first love with passion and intimacy that will enable greater unity, as Jesus prayed in John 17:

> I have given them the glory that you gave Me, that they may be one as We are one: I in them and You in Me. May they be brought to complete unity to let the world know that You sent Me and have loved them even as You have loved Me (John 17:22-23).

It was the dry season, and it had not rained for over three months. But that night, Randy Clark prophetically prayed for God to release the rain of His Spirit over Manuas. Instantly, lightning crashed; and within minutes, it began to pour. I stood on stage looking at between eight and ten thousand people in this church that had no walls. My Brazilian pastor spoke to me through a translator and said, "The Holy Spirit usually comes in power when it rains here."

Randy was trying to preach over the rain, but suddenly there was screaming and a loud commotion at the side of the church. A group of deaf and mute people was sitting where a wall should have been, and the rain was misting them. About eight people in this group began to speak and hear for the first time. Their interpreters were crying and praising Jesus.

Next, a blind man stood up and started yelling that he could see. Many others were falling out under the power of His presence.

We were witnessing Holy Spirit chaos. Randy turned to me and said, "We've lost control and God is here! Hallelujah!" It was amazing. There were sovereign healings occurring all over the place. My faith, expectations, and desire for more soared to another level that night. I was enjoying the manifestations of His love and presence, but I was soon to encounter a demonic presence from the kingdom of darkness.

Our Last Stop, Santarem

Then the dragon was enraged at the woman and went off to make war against the rest of her offspring—those who obey God's commandments and hold to the testimony of Jesus (Revelation 12:17).

The last stop on our mission trip in September 2001 was the small town of Santarem, located along the Amazon River in Northern Brazil. We were gripped by the feeling of heavy oppression as soon as we walked off the plane. The burden we felt in our spirits was so noticeable and very different from the spiritual feeling we had in Manaus.

I was told that Jesuits had founded Santarem in 1600, but it was immediately evident that the town had deviated far from its Christian roots. We arrived during the Festival of the Dolphins. It was believed that dolphins would manifest as men and have sexual relations with the women; therefore, free sex with whomever was acceptable behavior for the duration of the festival. We realized, like Dorothy in the *Wizard of Oz,* that we were "no longer in Kansas, Toto" when we witnessed sexual acts on the hotel lawn upon our arrival and discovered numerous condoms on the playground behind the hotel during our morning prayer walk the following day.

During prayer, we observed that the men intimidated the women. When we inquired about this, we learned that incest, rape, and molestation were rampant in Santarem. We quickly learned that immorality and witchcraft were responsible for much of the spiritual oppression in the town.

Knowing that these were the satan's weapons against the people and the Kingdom of God, Randy Clark, Mike Ellis, another deliverance minister, and I decided to confront these spirits of darkness directly during the service that night. Our plan was for Randy to "take authority" over the spirits while our team of 70 ministered to the individual needs of the people as they arose.

In Luke 10:19, Jesus says, *"I have given you authority over all power of the enemy, and you can walk among the snakes and scorpions and crush them. Nothing will injure you"* (NLT).

A pastor from the United States founded the church where we were scheduled to minister. He was killed in a plane crash prior to the completion of his vision to evangelize the Amazon River basin. His brother took his place to continue pursuing the vision. Before we dispatched to the church, we met in the hotel for prayer. The tension was palpable as we anticipated the spiritual battle that loomed ahead of us.

During this time, a conflict arose among four members of our team. I gathered them together and, exercising my pastoral authority, said that they would not be able to minister that night if they did not resolve their disagreement. Three of them displayed genuine forgiveness; however, one woman was not honest about letting go of her bitterness toward another member of the group.

An "open door," we would later learn, can also allow the entrance of demonic oppression. This is because the enemy wants to inhabit God's temple and we, as believers, are living temples.

In order to prevent the enemy from entering, we must be sure to keep the door closed. Any sin in our lives, including discord, gives the enemy an opportunity to enter the temple. In other words, it opens the door.

In spiritual warfare, it is important to have unity and harmony within a team that is ministering together. If someone on the team has been offended—harboring a spirit of offense—this can be an open door for disunity or discord, which impairs our ability to function in the full power and gifts of the Holy Spirit (see Gal. 5:19-21).

We put the incident behind us, arrived at the church, and worshiped together. Then Randy began to speak. As he took authority over all darkness and bound witchcraft, about 100 people fell to the floor simultaneously where they passed out and manifested in torment. It was obvious that the clash between the kingdom of darkness and the Kingdom of Light was real—and it was raging.

We began working like triage teams in a medical unit during a disaster. We carried out those who needed deliverance and had teams devoted to healing prayer. This experience contributed to the development of the Destiny Model of Prayer Ministry, which is described in Part III.

Suddenly, while engaged in prayer ministry, the woman who was unwilling to forgive her teammate was overcome by a spirit of torment and passed out. While she was lying on the floor, her male teammate, who was normally a calm businessman, was overcome by fear. As I ministered to the woman afflicted by the spirit of torment, the woman with whom she had the disagreement earlier that evening assisted me.

When we completed the ministry, complete forgiveness flowed between them. Since this event, the tormented woman has helped me to prepare many mission teams in subsequent years. This experience now serves as a powerful reminder to keep all doors closed so that a potentially serious episode like this is not repeated.[1]

The man who was gripped by a spirit of fear did not recover until we left Santarem. I was seated beside him on the flight out of Santarem and watched his countenance change abruptly from fear to freedom as soon as we flew out of Santarem's air space. He turned to me at this moment and simply said, "It's gone." He has had no further experiences of this gripping fear. I believe the Lord was showing me a territorial spirit similar to the one that Daniel experienced (see Dan. 10:13). In essence, different spirits of darkness may reside over different localities, which accounts for the different worldly problems that exist in various locations—Ephesians 6:10-18 speaks of these powers of darkness.

> *Finally, be strong in the Lord and in His mighty power. Put on the full armor of God so that you can take your stand against the devil's schemes. For our struggle is not against flesh and blood, but against the rulers, against the authorities, against the powers of this dark world and against the spiritual forces of evil in the heavenly realms* (Ephesians 6:10-12).

When I returned from Santarem, I read every book I could get my hands on about deliverance, sought advice on prayer ministry, and completed a certification program by Victorious Ministries Through Christ (VMCT). We began a prayer ministry program at our church in North Carolina and people began to come from all over to be set free from a variety of vexing problems, tormenting conditions, and spiritual lies that had previously prevented them from receiving inner healing and realizing their true identity.

Looking back, it is evident that God was using these experiences to equip us for a huge confrontation that was going to take place in Belem, Brazil, in September 2002.

But first, He led us to Mozambique.

ENDNOTE

1. I now require all who go on mission trips or do prayer ministry to undergo a session of personal prayer ministry first. I believe we all have wounds from life that require inner healing and greater spiritual truth. See John 15:26, John 16:13, James 5:16, and James 4:6-7.

CHAPTER 5

Mozambique

The Lord says, "I will guide you along the best pathway
for your life. I will advise you and watch over you (Psalm
32:8 NLT).

Mozambique, which has life expectancy and infant mortality
rates that are among the worst in the world, has been described
as the poorest nation on the planet. This sub-Saharan country on
the southeast border of Africa is where God completely broke my
heart for the poor.

On November 11, 2001, while attending a conference in the
States, Heidi Baker prayed for me. My journal entry from that
day says, "I, Tom Hauser, died today when Heidi Baker prayed
for me...Lord, I want to carry Your glory, no matter what the
cost." Heidi and her husband, Rolland, are missionaries and
have dedicated their lives to serving the poorest of the poor and

are now responsible for the planting of over 10,000 churches and the care of thousands of orphans in Africa.

Our church planned a trip to Maputo, Mozambique, along with Randy Clark's organization, Global Awakening, to minister with Heidi and Rolland. Randy Clark and Charles Stock (senior pastor of Life Center in Harrisburg, Pennsylvania) visited our North Carolina church prior to our mission trip and prophesied over me. Charles said, "New, exciting, and wild experiences are coming." Randy said, "Raise him up to the nations—Africa." Several years before this, my wife, Ginny, had a vision that she and I were in a distant land with dark-skinned children singing all around. This vision was fulfilled on this trip as we traveled into the African bush.

These prophetic words became clearer when we baptized Muslim converts in crocodile rivers and ministered in the wild bush in Africa during trips to Mozambique and Tanzania. It still moves my heart to reminisce about my wife dancing for hours in the dirt with the children of Mozambique in praise of Jesus.

Our church's team ministered on the streets of Maputo, in the prison, and in the garbage dump, where forgotten families live among the stench. We were completely undone by the plight of the people who lived in the garbage dump and the starving children we encountered in the bush. Our hearts were so broken for the impoverished converts that we knew we had to offer more. The gospel of the love of Jesus compelled us to be His hands and His feet.

One of our missions while in Mozambique was to provide relief to the pastors living in the isolated area of Mutara, an area that had been devastated by flooding of the Zambezi River. After a harrowing, eight-hour drive on severely damaged dirt roads, we arrived at our destination. There are simply no words to describe the devastation that awaited us there. I cried for hours then, and I cry again now as I recall the starvation, sickness, and destitution we witnessed there. Desperate mothers brought baby after baby to Ginny to pray for healing—they were all so sick and so hungry. They were dying of starvation, malaria, and AIDS.

Rolland Baker, Tom Jones, a pastor from a church in Florida, and I preached while Ginny prayed for and comforted the women and their children. I shared the love of Jesus with them and explained that no other god or devil could help them—Jesus is their only hope. The people began to place their objects of witchcraft—bracelets and amulets they believed kept away evil spirits—at the altar to be burned as they gave their hearts to Jesus.

The miracles we experienced in Mozambique involved a transformation of hearts among our team members as well as those who were waiting back home. Our congregation was so moved by our testimonies that we raised $80,000, built two houses, bought a Land Rover, and sent four full-time missionaries to Mozambique the following year. Two of the missionaries still serve there today. Now in their sixth year, they have begun serving in a Muslim village in Northern Mozambique. Our youngest daughter, Laura, also decided to serve in Mozambique for a year as a missionary by running the horse program for orphans in Pemba. While there, she met and later married one of Heidi and Rolland's adopted sons, Elvis Lopez.

The work God did in our hearts in Mozambique did not vanish when we returned to the States. A wealthy businessman from our church had frequently supported our missionary efforts by contributing financially, but his heart had never been into personally serving. However, he agreed to go on this particular trip.

Although he had never preached before, he led 20 inmates to the Lord while preaching in a prison in Maputo, Mozambique.

When we returned to his million dollar home overlooking the Intracoastal Waterway, he was reduced to tears when his wife brought him a plate of eggs sunny-side up. He recalls that all he could do was cry. Jesus got hold of his heart in Mozambique and continued to possess it until his dying day. I was with him at the hospital during his last days, and we spoke of our days in a faraway land where Jesus made us acutely aware of the needs of the poor and the broken. In the midst of this, we somehow became more alive and at peace with the previously under-appreciated blessings of our own lives.

God got hold of another heart after Maputo, the heart of my secretary, Pat Walls.

Phil and Pat

Pat Walls is my administrative assistant and the wife of my close friend, Phil. Her formative years were spent in the New York and New Jersey area, and her idea of "roughing it" is a room in a three-star hotel. While we were making plans to go to Mozambique, she made it clear that she had no desire to venture into a third world country, especially not the continent of Africa.

One night, Pat had a dream. In that dream, she clearly saw three numbers. The following day, she described her dream to me and another pastor. We both chimed in at the same time, "Check the latitude and longitude of those numbers." The three numbers were the exact locations of the two places we had mission trips planned for that year: Maputo, Mozambique, and Belem, Brazil.

Pat relented and stayed in a tent in Mozambique. She says, "Only for Jesus could this happen. It had to be God!" Pat's husband,

Phil, had previously received a word of knowledge that he would build a house for Heidi Baker. While we were in Mozambique, Heidi discovered a young girl living on the streets who was forced into prostitution for survival and had become pregnant. The girl accepted Jesus into her life, and Heidi needed a home to take her in. Heidi went to Phil, a construction contractor, and asked him to build a house on the orphanage compound. Our team gladly assisted the local men in building the house. This former homeless prostitute became a "momma" to the orphans that Heidi gathered from the streets. God is truly amazing and His ways are not our ways (see Isa. 55:8).

Through the visions, words of knowledge, and experiences of Phil, Pat, and others, our team learned to listen, observe, and obey. This was a timely teaching, as my life would depend upon my ability to listen carefully to the Holy Spirit's guidance on our next mission trip to the Amazon region of Brazil.

CHAPTER 6

Back in Brazil

Stay alert! Watch out for your great enemy, the devil. He prowls around like a roaring lion, looking for someone to devour. Stand firm against him, and be strong in your faith. Remember that your Christian brothers and sisters all over the world are going through the same kind of suffering you are (1 Peter 5:8-9 NLT).

We returned home from Mozambique at the end of August 2002, and the 16 missionaries from this trip inspired another team to return to Belem, Brazil, a month later. We would be joining Randy Clark and Bill Johnson, who were planning to host a conference with 20,000 attendees as well as minister to 70 churches in Northern Brazil. Randy expressed his pleasure that our 15 experienced team members were going join the Global Awakening team of nearly 60.

The Armor Division Is Formed

Two days before I was to depart for Brazil, I received a frantic phone call from one of my key intercessors who was crying. He said that he had been up all night praying for me and had a revelation that satan was going to try to kill me on this trip. He wasn't sure if I should go.

After hanging up the phone, I prayed about whether I should tell my wife what I had just heard, as I knew it would worry her. I decided to tell her and afterward we prayed together. Through prayer, we determined that I was to go, but to listen carefully to the Holy Spirit for guidance.

Another intercessor then told me that the Lord told her to pray for me for three hours each and every day of the two weeks that I would be gone. This knowledge provided me with inner peace. God is good and faithful!

Our team of 15 arrived in Belem, Brazil. Randy Clark greeted us and asked me if I would run the deliverance tent during the conference. We had learned from the previous years that many people were involved in witchcraft in Brazil and would have demonic manifestations during worship and preaching. So Randy asked our team to train several hundred Brazilians to escort anyone who was being tormented by demons to the deliverance tent. This plan was devised to minimize the disruption in the main conference so that attendees could listen to and respond to the altar call for salvation while we provided deliverance for those in need.

Recalling the warning I received before my departure, my first reaction was, "Aha! This is satan's plan to kill me." I had never been asked to do anything this "big" before, and I was concerned that our efforts to defeat the kingdom of darkness would be dangerous if we were not working within the confines of the Lord's plan for us. I had to be sure this was the Lord's will before I agreed to have our team involved.

I responded to Randy, "Why would the Brazilians want a non-Brazilian doing their deliverance? If Pastor Paulo, the head of the Brazilian Foursquare Churches, asks me, I will pray and see if I should do it."

Randy arranged for us to have lunch with Pastor Paulo. During our meal, Pastor Paulo said that they needed direction for deliverance and then he asked me to run it. I had seen how the Brazilians handled demonic manifestations in the past. They would pull the person's hair, hit them, or pour water on them in an effort to make them "snap out of it." I wasn't sure how I would oversee such a bizarre deliverance effort.

I returned to the hotel and called Steve Mattis, a friend and pastor at the Vineyard Church in Wilmington. I knew he rarely answered the phone, so I was relieved when he picked up and I heard his voice on the other end of the line. I relayed my predicament to him, including the warning I had received before leaving for Brazil. Pastor Steve began to prophesy over me through the phone. He said, "You have been prepared for such a time as this." He then said, "You should do it." I hung up the phone and lay on the floor crying out to God, "Lord, I will go and do what You say. Show me the strategy to defeat the enemy."

Then I began to prepare for the task ahead of me. I got a clear picture of the Lord's strategy. Knowing that 20,000 attendees were expected, I planned to train at least 200 Brazilians to bring the tormented to the deliverance tent. Next, I would isolate a specific area for deliverance and assign teams of two with a translator. I would make sure the area was well lit and surrounded by intercessors. Then the entire team would walk the perimeter of the stadium, as well as the deliverance area, seven times—in my mind, I had a picture of Joshua and Israel marching around the city seven times before the battle of Jericho—while anointing it with oil to break the power of witchcraft. (I later learned that a Macumba witch was assigned to this stadium, which was considered Macumba's domain at that time. But God was about to change this!)

The Lord warned me that satan would send his "plants" to disrupt the service or harm the team or worse—to try to kill us! He told me that I was not to minister to everyone who came to the tent. I was to be discerning of good and evil (see Heb. 5:14).

As I entered the elevator to descend, I felt my mission was well-defined and I was elated, but nervous. Believing I was alone in the elevator, I cried out loud to the Lord for help. Immediately, I felt two large hands on my shoulders and fell to my knees under the pressure. I believe a large angel was in the elevator with me as I proceeded to cry out for the Lord's goodness, grace, and direction. I sought out Randy and told him I would fulfill his request to run the deliverance tent.

I spent a full day training a team of 250 Brazilians, along with my team of 15 from Wilmington. Toward the end of the day, I was weary from the long day of training, but God was about to energize me.

The Blind Lady

An old man led a woman in her late 70s into the church. I could tell that she was blind by the way he was guiding her. They approached the altar where I was teaching. I stopped and waited while the translator asked them what they wanted. They said that if I would pray for her, she would receive her sight. I thought, *Oh great, there's no pressure in front of 250 people.* At that time, my faith was even smaller than a mustard seed!

I walked over and laid my hands over her eyes praying, "Lord God, You said the blind would see, the lame would walk, and the deaf would hear. In the name of Jesus, I command her eyes to see." When I pulled my hand from her eyes, she went wild. She touched the man's face next to her, and my translator went crazy with excitement. He said he had never seen a miracle. My faith and energy level shot through the roof. This was the perfect ending to an amazing day. The newly trained group received confirmation that God was with us with supernatural power. Miracles broke out in the crowd. My team member Phil Walls prayed and two blind people received their sight. What a God we serve!

I noticed that the man who had brought the woman to the altar was acting very stoic and low-key about everything. I thought this was odd since the woman had just had her vision miraculously restored. I admit that I found his nonchalant behavior a little annoying. When the celebration quieted down, the woman told me that this man was her husband and that he did not know Jesus Christ personally.

With the translator's assistance, I asked him if he was pleased with what Jesus had done. He responded, "uh-huh." I persisted, "Did you see the power of Jesus?" He replied, "Yes." Then I asked him if he wanted to receive Jesus and he replied, "No." I grew more irritated with him. He was so old looking, and I thought he could die any day. So I said, "You could die on the walk home and then where would you be?" He remained quiet for a moment and then replied, "OK, I'll receive Jesus." My translator led him to the Lord.

I found out later that the translator was a pastor from the Assemblies of God Church, and he had been a missionary to

Mozambique. By witnessing this miracle, an opportunity arose for us to minister later to the Assemblies of God churches in Northern Brazil. Our God is truly an amazing God!

The Intercessors

On the night of the conference it rained for hours, and I expected a small crowd due to the poor weather. But the weather did not seem to deter the people from coming; we estimated that 18,000 people were there. The multitude of people stood shoulder to shoulder in a soccer field waiting to enter the stadium. I asked the deliverance team to pray for the translators and intercessors that were assigned to the deliverance tent. There were about 800 intercessors from 70 Foursquare Churches in Brazil, and they had prayed and fasted for 30 days prior to the meeting.

The 800 intercessors, who were all wearing white shirts and black pants or skirts, stood in two lines, and we walked through the tunnel they formed as we entered the stadium along with the 18,000 attendees. It was an impressive sight.

My friend Phil Walls, who had been a combat and demolition soldier in Vietnam, was responsible for patrolling the perimeter of the deliverance area to make sure the area was secure from any threats. Phil is not afraid of anything, and I trust him with my life. On previous mission trips he had been given the name Doctor Fogo, the Doctor of Fire, because he had wild results whenever he laid his hands on someone and imparted the fire of the Holy Spirit to them.

I asked Phil to gather the intercessors in the deliverance area and invite the Holy Spirit to come join us. WOW! The Lord came, but about six of the intercessors exhibited demonic manifestations. From this experience, we learned to pray for the intercessors *before* they are asked to pray for our deliverance team. We excused the six of them to sign up for their own deliverance and did not use their prayer services for the deliverance team.

Olsa

What happened the next day made Randy Clark's ministry well known among the members of the Foursquare churches in Belem. A lady named Olsa, who was involved in Macumba witchcraft and had been a prostitute for more than 20 years, had been saved six months earlier. She was a large, powerful, tough woman; and every time the spirit of God fell upon a worship service, she would have demonic manifestations that were significant enough to completely disrupt the service. Weighing over 300 pounds, she was too large for anybody to hold her down or remove her from the service. Out of fear, nobody would sit near her in church.

While we were worshiping in the stadium, Olsa had demonic manifestations. The crowd parted and a path was cleared for her to be escorted to the deliverance area; but six Brazilian men were thrown off of her, and she was going wild. Olsa began to run full speed toward the deliverance area with wild eyes. She was clearly tormented.

Someone opened the door to the deliverance area, and I looked up to see her charging at my team member Nick and me. I quickly remembered a lesson I had learned on a previous trip and said, "Paz, en nome de Jesus," which means "Peace, in the name of Jesus." She fell unconscious to the floor, and I thought, *OK, that works.* Jesus' name is powerful! Nick looked at me and said, "Now that's cool!"

For the next three nights, Olsa would get in line and wait for her deliverance. I was waiting for the Lord to tell me what to do, because I thought she might be one of the "plants" from the enemy. On the final night she was out there again, waiting patiently. Three members of my team asked me to please minister to her this time. I felt the Holy Spirit confirm this.

So, with Olsa's pastor present, my team began a six-hour deliverance. We carefully dealt with unforgiveness and confession in order to avoid wild manifestations. We saw things during Olsa's deliverance that we had never seen before. Her skin broke out in hives and began to tear open. As she would tearfully forgive and confess, her wounds closed over and healed. After she had been set free from many demons, she became so beautiful and peaceful.

Olsa's miraculous healing was so remarkable to her pastor that he would retell the story numerous times; consequently, Randy Clark's Ministry for Emotional Healing becoming widely recognized and sought after in the region. We have been invited back to Belen on two additional ministry trips thus far.

Hand-to-Hand Combat

Ana Paula was born into a family of Macumba witches who forced her into prostitution at a young age. She came to the healing tent at the age of 15 with a tormented countenance. Randy and his translator, Claris, laid hands on her in prayer. She instantly fell to the ground and began screaming and vomiting blood.

Claris, a native Brazilian who had participated in deliverances in this region before, recalled that she had seen this happen to other people who had eaten food that was dedicated to idols during Macumba rituals; their stomachs were cursed. They prayed for peace over Ana Paula and her symptoms abated. The ministry team asked her if she wanted to be free from demonic oppression and whether she trusted in Jesus Christ as Lord and Savior. Ana

Paula replied yes to both questions and it was arranged that she would return to the deliverance tent the next day.

Ana Paula returned the following day, and Claris, along with several members of our team, began to minister to her. She became so tormented that she could not speak. The demons were choking her. At one point, she became almost comatose. Jesus describes this in the gospels as being dead (see Mark 9:26). Claris became frustrated because Ana Paula was unable to confess or forgive due to her inability to speak. Claris asked for my help, so I asked the Holy Spirit, "Lord, we have a woman who is saved and wants to be free, what do we do?" The answer I believe I received was strange: "hand-to-hand combat." I interpreted this to mean that we should get close and use physical approaches.

So I gathered seven team members together and we, along with Claris, spent the next three to four hours in hand-to-hand combat. I cast out every negative spirit I could think of, and we witnessed many things we had never seen before. Ana Paula elevated like a board, despite several team members sitting on her. I know this sounds strange, but I am reporting what we experienced!

Although Ana Paula only spoke Portuguese, at one point a demon within her spoke aloud in English. He spoke directly to another team member, Mark, and said, "I am going to kill you." Mark turned to me and said, "Did you hear that?" Mark looked concerned about the death threat, but I told him not to worry because demons always lie. (Mark is still alive and well today!)

When I couldn't think of any other demons to cast out, I asked the Holy Spirit what to do next. He replied, "All pray in tongues." We did as we were asked; about 20 minutes later, the demon spoke in English again and said, "It is getting hot in here." We were excited because we knew the fire of the Holy Spirit was burning out the demon. We continued praying in tongues, and about 10 minutes later, the demon said, "We are leaving."

Immediately Ana Paula came out of her comatose, rigid state and exclaimed in Portuguese, "I am free!" She returned to the tent the next day to thank us. We were all amazed. The tormented prostitute had been transformed into a beautiful, peaceful 15-year-old child. God is so amazing!

I have given you authority...to overcome all the power of the enemy (Luke 10:19).

The Enemy Arrives

During the conference, a man came to the tent seeking deliverance. He was explaining to two team members that he had been involved in Macumba sacrifices and had been blood sacrificed to the devil. The men called me over. When I approached him, I could see death in his eyes; they were cold, dark, and not moving. The temperature seemed to drop about 10 degrees when I stood near him. I recalled Hebrews 5:14, "the mature, who by constant use have trained themselves to distinguish good from evil." My senses were crying out, "EVIL!" Because it was already late in the evening, I told him to return the next day and we would see about ministry.

When we arrived the next day, he was standing by himself, wearing the same clothes as the night before, and was the first one in line. Once again I felt the presence of evil. I detected no signs of repentance or desire for freedom, just evil. I had heard of cases where those who are demonized seek a Christian deliverance to gain more power. This is based on the Scripture that says if a demon is cast out, seven other spirits, more evil than the original one, may return (see Matt. 12:45).

Although I wasn't entirely certain of this man's intent, it was clear to me that the Holy Spirit was saying, "Do NOT minister to him." We began doing deliverance in the tent while he stood watching and waiting. I noticed that he was praying and writing while focusing on one of our teams and then the next. When three of our translators became nauseous and sick, I knew he was cursing our teams. A righteous anger welled up inside of me. I summoned Phil Walls, the perimeter control leader, to the tent. I shared my perceptions with Phil and told him to ask this man to leave; he could follow up with a Brazilian pastor later.

Phil went out to the man while I continued to minister. A little while later, one of our team members, who is a registered nurse, came running up to me shouting, "Phil is having a heart attack!" I knew this was a curse. The man we were asking to leave was sending a death spirit to Phil.

I ran over to Phil; he was ashen and "scary" looking. The guy was standing there with a mocking look on his face, and I felt the Holy Spirit rise within me for war. But I turned my attention back to Phil and said in a loud voice, "In the name of Jesus, I cut you free from death and witchcraft." Later, Phil told me he felt like a large hand was gripping his heart. When I said those words, he felt the hand release. Immediately after I spoke those words, Phil's color returned to normal and he no longer looked "scary."

I then focused my attention back on the guy. I bound his power of witchcraft and commanded him to leave the stadium. We locked eyes and we both knew that his dark power was no match for the power and authority of Jesus. My emotions were mixed. I was angry, but I also felt sad for him. It was also exhilarating to feel the power of Jesus and to experience the reality of God as our Protector. This power was something we would come to rely on in our future battles in Argentina, Mozambique, Tanzania, England, Spain, and other mission fields.

Phil Walls, who is such a trooper, stood up after all this and escorted the defeated satanist to the boundary of the stadium. Phil reported that when he reached the perimeter, the guy fell to the ground and had a demonic manifestation. He was writhing in the dirt like a snake. Despite two future trips to Belem, we never encountered him again. We don't know whether he lived or died, but I pray that he became free from the tormenting control of satan.

After this trip, Randy Clark began referring to our team from Wilmington, North Carolina, as the Armor Division of Global Awakening. We used God's teaching, the Holy Spirit's guidance, and our dramatic experiences ministering on the mission fields to develop the Destiny Model of Deliverance that we share with you in the next part of *Breaking Free*.

Breaking Free

The model for deliverance that follows is a biblically based framework to safely set yourself and others free. We have found, on many continents, that following this approach will protect the people you minister to as well as the team participating in the ministry.

Part II

Principles to Set You Free

I tell you the truth, anyone who has faith in Me will do what I have been doing. He will do even greater things than these, because I am going to the Father. **And I will do whatever you ask in My name**, *so that the Son may bring glory to the Father. You may ask Me for anything in My name, and I will do it* (John 14:12-14).

My desire is that God will raise up warriors to defeat the works of darkness and help others get free (see 1 John 3:8; John 14:12; Mark 16:17). My desire is that you will be one of these warriors. If so, your services will likely be utilized in some sort of prayer ministry.

Prayer Ministry is the art of using prayer—with authority in the name of Jesus—to obtain healing and deliverance for yourself or others. Prayer ministry is based on what Jesus did and His command for us to go and do likewise. Part of this ministry is confronting the darkness in a person's life. But it is important to keep the focus on Jesus and His Kingdom, not on satan and his minions (see Luke 10:17-21). It is exciting and wonderful to see the demonic influence in a person's life broken and to see demons flee because of the great name of Jesus. But this is just one part of deliverance; there is more to prayer ministry than this.

Prayer ministry is also an opportunity to confront erroneous beliefs that interfere with an individual's ability to achieve the full purpose God has for them. Erroneous beliefs can open the doorway for darkness to negatively influence a person's life.

In Romans 12:2, we read that God transforms people by changing the way they think. The Holy Spirit's guidance is paramount to prayer ministry, because in order to transform thoughts, we need the revelation of truth. The prayer ministry team's purpose is to seek such revelation from the Holy Spirit for the individual receiving ministry.

Prayer ministry can also help a tormented individual find peace. The mind, which is part of the soul, is capable of being deceived. When the mind is in charge, not subservient to the Spirit, and it believes lies, it may cause a person to fall into temptation or to lose his or her peace. As a man or a woman believes in his or her heart, so it is (see Prov. 23:7). This is true regardless of whether they believe the truth or a lie. The lens through which a person looks impacts everything they see. When we restore the spirit to its proper position of authority over our soul—our emotions and intellect—the truth becomes evident. Only then can an individual acquire true peace (see Gal. 5:16-25).

Setting another free is exhilarating, but it is important to remember that all the glory belongs to the Lord. Prayer ministry members do not accomplish deliverance; freedom ultimately comes from an intimate encounter with Jesus Christ. That being said, the Lord is looking for additional warriors to become prayer ministry members. Read on to learn the basic beliefs that underlie the Destiny Model of Prayer Ministry.

CHAPTER 7

Believe in God

You may be thinking that prayer ministry is a job for a few select, highly anointed believers. But this is not biblical, nor is it true. According to Scripture, all believers are given the ability, even a responsibility, to call upon God, through Jesus, to perform signs and wonders. This is described in the Great Commission:

Jesus said:

> Go into all the world and preach the Good News to everyone. ...These miraculous signs will accompany those who believe: They will cast out demons in My name, and they will speak in new languages. They will be able to handle snakes with safety, and if they drink anything poisonous, it won't hurt them. They will be able to place their hands on the sick, and they will be healed (Mark 16:15, 17-18 NLT).

Many Christians have reduced the Great Commission to being "saved." Have ever heard someone ask, "Are you saved?" They are wondering if you have heard the Good News that Jesus Christ is God and is the Way, the Truth, and the Life, and that you have accepted Him into your heart. But the full meaning of the word "saved" has been lost in translation. The Greek word for saved is *sozo,* and it is much more complex and wonderful than today's Christian definition of saved as described above.

The word *sozo* is used more than 110 times in the New Testament. It is a Greek verb or action word meaning to be saved or rescued out from under satan's power and restored into the wholeness of God's order and well-being. It is used to mean saved in the sense of being saved from eternal punishment for sin. It is used to mean to be healed of disease. It is used to mean to be delivered from demonic oppression. In fact, it can mean all three of these at the same time. It is also the verb used when someone is raised from the dead. To be *sozo,* is to be saved completely. In other words, God intends for all believers to receive salvation, health, and deliverance. This is what it means to be completely saved or *sozo.*

The Great Commission invites all believers to save others completely by performing miraculous healings and deliverances in Jesus' name. If you want to join this Great Commission, the first step is to become a believer.

Is God Real?

If you are not sure whether God exists and is sovereign, or if Jesus really is the Son of God who was sacrificed for our sins, do not worry. Simply ask God to prove it. Say the following out loud right now, "God, I want to believe in You, but I don't know if You are real. If You are real, please show me!"

Ask and it will be given to you; seek and you will find; knock and the door will be opened to you. For

everyone who asks receives; he who seeks finds; and to him who knocks, the door will be opened (Luke 11:9-10).

The Prayer of Salvation

Once this prayer has been answered, and you are sure that Jesus is real, you can pray a prayer of salvation:

Father, I am truly sorry for all the times I have fallen short of Your perfect will for my life. I am sorry for all the times I have sinned by doing the wrong thing or by not doing what is right. I want to change. I choose now to turn away from my past sinful life toward You. Please forgive me and help me to change my ways. Help me also to forgive those who have hurt me. I believe that Your Son Jesus Christ died for my sins and was resurrected from the dead. I ask Jesus to become the Lord of my life and to rule in my heart from now on. Please send Your Holy Spirit to guide me and to help me to do Your will for the rest of my life. In Jesus' name, I pray. Amen.

Be certain that you verbalize the prayer of salvation and that you believe it with all your heart before attempting to perform deliverance. The Bible provides an example of the harm that can befall those who attempt to cast out demons without the proper authority that is granted to all believers who have accepted Jesus into their hearts.

Some Jews who went around driving out evil spirits tried to invoke the name of the Lord Jesus over those who were demon-possessed. They would say, "In the name of Jesus, whom Paul preaches, I command you to come out." One day the evil spirit answered them, "Jesus I know, and I know Paul, but who are you?" Then the man who had the evil spirit jumped on them and overpowered them all (Acts 19:13,15-16).

Expect the Miraculous

Now that you are a fellow believer, you need to know the believers' job description as outlined in John 14:12, *"I tell you the truth, anyone who has faith in me will do what I have been doing. He will do even greater things than these, because I am going to the Father."*

First John 3:8 says that, *"The reason the Son of God appeared was to destroy the devil's work."* This means that we, as believers, are called to destroy the works of the devil, whose job description is to steal, kill, and destroy (see John 10:10).

And in order to fulfill this role, we need to perform miraculous healings and deliverances.

After reviewing these Scriptures, you can eliminate doubt and continue in faith. God has given all believers, including you, the power to perform miracles in Jesus' name. As you co-labor with the Lord in the process of deliverance, expect the miraculous!

CHAPTER 8

Know the Enemy

So humble yourselves before God. Resist the devil, and he will flee from you. Come close to God, and God will come close to you... (James 4:7-8 NLT).

Although I do not encourage you to focus on demons or the kingdom of darkness, it is important to know who the enemy is. The Bible demonstrates that satan is the god of this world (see 2 Cor. 4:4), and the ruler of this world (see John 14:30), and the whole world is under the rule of the evil one (see 1 John 5:19). Satan informed Jesus (see Luke 4:5-6) that all the power and riches had been handed over to him, and he could give it to anyone whom he chooses. Although satan is the master of deception, he was speaking the truth in this case.

The Bible describes how satan came to reign over the world in Revelation 12:

And war broke out in heaven: Michael and his angels fought with the dragon; and the dragon and his angels fought, but they did not prevail, nor was a place found for them in heaven any longer. So the great dragon was cast out, that serpent of old, called the Devil and Satan, who deceives the whole world; he was cast to the earth, and his angels were cast out with him.

Then I heard a loud voice saying in heaven, "Now salvation, and strength, and the kingdom of our God, and the power of His Christ have come, for the accuser of our brethren, who accused them before our God day and night, has been cast down. And they overcame him by the blood of the Lamb and by the word of their testimony, and they did not love their lives to the death. Therefore rejoice, O heavens, and you who dwell in them! Woe to the inhabitants of the earth and the sea! For the devil has come down to you, having great wrath, because he knows that he has a short time."

Now when the dragon saw that he had been cast to the earth, he persecuted the woman who gave birth to the male Child. But the woman was given two wings of a great eagle, that she might fly into the wilderness to her place, where she is nourished for a time and times and half a time, from the presence of the serpent. So the serpent spewed water out of his mouth like a flood after the woman, that he might cause her to be carried away by the flood. But the earth helped the woman, and the earth opened its mouth and swallowed up the flood which the dragon had spewed out of his mouth. And the dragon was enraged with the woman, and he went to make war with the rest of her offspring, who keep the commandments of God and have the testimony of Jesus Christ (Revelation 12:7-17 NKJV).

This Scripture passage reveals that satan has declared war on all who keep God's commandments and have confessed that they belonged to Christ. (See also Ezekiel 28:11-19 and Isaiah 14:12-15.)

The apostle Paul tells us that the conflicts we experience in this world are not a result of the people we see before us, but are a result of unseen spiritual influences and manipulation. His words:

For our struggle is not against flesh and blood, but against the rulers, against the authorities, against the powers of this dark world and against the spiritual forces of evil in the heavenly realms (Ephesians 6:12).

Scripture makes it clear that the devil will attempt to harm us, but is equally clear that we are not to lie down in defeat, but to take a stand and resist him.

Stay alert! Watch out for your great enemy, the devil. He prowls around like a roaring lion, looking for someone to devour. Stand firm against him, and be strong in your faith. Remember that your Christian brothers and sisters all over the world are going through the same kind of suffering you are (1 Peter 5:8-9 NLT).

So how are we to fight against spiritual forces? Paul instructs us to:

Therefore put on the full armor of God, so that when the day of evil comes, you may be able to stand your ground, and after you have done everything, to stand. Stand firm then, with the belt of truth buckled around your waist, with the breastplate of righteousness in place, and with your feet fitted with the readiness that comes from the gospel of peace. In addition to all this, take up the shield of faith, with which you can extinguish all the flaming arrows of the evil one. Take the helmet of salvation and the sword of the Spirit, which is the word of God. And pray in the Spirit on all occasions with all kinds of prayers and requests. With this in mind, be alert and always keep on praying for all the saints (Ephesians 6:13-18).

Once we are armed with faith, righteousness, the knowledge of our salvation, *sozo*, and the Word of God in our hearts, we are ready to engage in prayer ministry by utilizing the sword of the spirit and the power of prayer. Jesus says He gave them power and authority to cast out demons and heal all diseases (see Luke 9:1). Jesus gave us authority over all the enemy's power so that we could walk among snakes and scorpions—the demonic realm—and crush them. Nothing will injure us (see Luke 10:17-19). I encourage you to find a warrior partner. Jesus did not send His disciples out alone. In Luke 9-10, Jesus sends out the 12 apostles and then the 72 disciples; they are all sent in pairs.

Victory

Whenever a demon is cast out, the Kingdom of God has manifested in our midst (see Matt. 12:28).

Then one was brought to Him who was demon-possessed, blind and mute; and He healed him, so that the blind and mute man both spoke and saw. And all the multitudes were amazed and said, "Could this be the Son of David?"

Now when the Pharisees heard it they said, "This fellow does not cast out demons except by Beelzebub, the ruler of the demons."

But Jesus knew their thoughts, and said to them: "Every kingdom divided against itself is brought to desolation, and every city or house divided against itself will not stand. If Satan casts out Satan, he is divided against himself. How then will his kingdom stand? And if I cast out demons by Beelzebub, by whom do your sons cast them out? Therefore they shall be your judges. But if I cast out demons by the Spirit of God, surely the kingdom of God has come upon you. Or how can one enter a strong man's house and plunder his goods, unless he first binds the strong man? And then he will plunder his house. He who is not with Me is against Me, and he who does not gather with Me scatters abroad.

"Therefore I say to you, every sin and blasphemy will be forgiven men, but the blasphemy against the Spirit will not be forgiven men. Anyone who speaks a word against the Son of Man, it will be forgiven him; but whoever speaks against the Holy Spirit, it will not be forgiven him, either in this age or in the age to come.

"Either make the tree good and its fruit good, or else make the tree bad and its fruit bad; for a tree is known by its fruit. Brood of vipers! How can you, being evil, speak good things? For out of the abundance of the heart the mouth speaks. A good man out of the good treasure of his heart brings forth good things, and an evil man out of the evil treasure brings forth evil things. But I say to you that for every idle word men may speak, they will give account of it in the day of judgment. For by your words you will be justified, and by your words you will be condemned" (Matthew 12:22-37 NKJV).

Deliverance demonstrates that the Kingdom of God is superior to the defeated kingdom of darkness.

Sally's Story

A woman, whom I will call Sally, was a church intercessor, and she came to me asking for prayer. She also informed me that recently when she tried to pray "in the Spirit," she would curse violently. She also expressed that she held great animosity toward her husband. I quickly set an appointment for her to receive ministry.

Sally had been a Christian for nearly 20 years. She was a mother of three, married, held a PhD in nursing and was a university professor. She was not only a brilliant individual, but she also radiated a sunny personality. She was active in church and a faithful intercessor. She was well-read and had studied many books on true intimacy with the Lord. By all outward appearances, she seemed perfectly fine.

Sally hesitantly came in for her pre-prayer interview, as she was developing "cold feet." Only after hearing several life-changing testimonials from others did she change her mind. The pre-interview helps me assess each person's need and true desire for prayer ministry. I explained the Destiny Model process to her. I then asked her specific questions. Immediately, I gained insight into her situation. First of all, I discovered her husband was not a Christian and wasn't supportive of her faith.

Second, she was from another country known for its anti-Christian beliefs. Third, for many years she had received secular counseling where she had spent thousands of dollars seeking answers for her anger toward her husband. Fourth, she experienced tormenting thoughts that caused her great anxiety and rage. Her highly educated logic, however, could not free her from this anguish. I briefly prayed with her and scheduled her prayer ministry appointment.

Two weeks later, with four to five hours set aside for uninterrupted ministry time, I, along with my ministry partner, met with Sally. She seemed to be backstroking as she informed us that she no longer needed prayer ministry. She said that after receiving prayer during the pre-interview, she was no longer tormented and that her husband was doing wonderfully. In fact, she exclaimed that he was now serving her breakfast in bed! I suspected that the demonic influences had taken cover for a strategic advantage. I mentioned that since the three of us were there and scheduled for ministry, why not follow through? Sally agreed.

Sally began by sharing her list of forgiveness items and began her confession process. Soon the Holy Spirit brought forth a revelation through an illustration given by my ministry partner and a word of knowledge I shared. My partner saw a burlap bag full of black seeds from a long ago time in history; it was not a modern-day image. Simultaneously, I heard in my spirit, "generational witchcraft." After sharing this knowledge with Sally, she agreed that she was aware of previous ancestral witchcraft in her family history. She went on to inform us that her mother had been a medium.

Sally continued to explain that even while she was a Christian, she had consulted psychics with her mother. However, she indicated that it had occurred several years prior to our meeting and that she had already privately asked for forgiveness of generational witchcraft and her involvement with psychics years earlier. I pressed ahead and asked her if she would be willing to renounce those things once again. Even though she felt that she had previously confessed those matters, and considered them history and irrelevant, she consented to renouncing the involvement her family and ancestors had with witchcraft. Scripture tells us to let everything be established with two or three witnesses. There is life and death in your tongue.

As soon as Sally spoke the words, "I renounce genera..." she arose, glared at me, and started to grab me. I was forced to restrain her to protect myself. She began speaking in a deep male voice,

"She is mine; I am high level and you can't have her." I spoke back with authority, "I know Someone higher than you—His name is Jesus, and I have authority over you. You can't have her, she has confessed, and you're a trespasser!" The demonic spirit began to whine, "Where will I go?" I commanded, "Go to the dry places Jesus created for you." The spirit then said, "OK," and left her. Finally, Sally, deeply embarrassed, looked at me and began to apologize profusely for the episode that had just taken place.

Soon after, she presented the church with a sizable donation. She expressed that she had wasted years and countless dollars in secular therapy; she believed the four hours she spent in prayer ministry were extremely cost effective! Sally could not contain her gratitude and joy over her deliverance. She stood before the church body and proclaimed her testimony of God's supernatural healing power. Today, she no longer suffers from torment. She continues to teach at the university and heads a successful Sunday school program.

Her witness serves as a powerful testimony of the stark reality of the demonic realm and doors that can be opened by our ancestors. Sin can also give these dark influences authorization by our own rebellion. These sins are defilements that become doorways to torment.

Demons Torment People

The Gospels provide several accounts of people who were tormented by demons. When these demons were confronted and commanded to leave, the individuals were healed of their tormenting conditions. In the Gospel of Mark, Jesus healed a man from insanity and self-mutilation:

So they arrived at the other side of the lake, in the region of the Gerasenes. When Jesus climbed out of the boat, a man possessed by an evil spirit came out from a cemetery to meet him. This man lived among the burial caves and could no longer be restrained, even with a chain. Whenever he was put into chains and shackles—as he often was—he snapped the chains from his wrists and smashed the shackles. No one was strong enough to subdue him. Day and night he wandered among the burial caves and in the hills, howling and cutting himself with sharp stones.

When Jesus was still some distance away, the man saw Him, ran to meet Him, and bowed low before Him. With a shriek, he screamed, "Why are You interfering with me, Jesus, Son of the Most High God? In the name of God, I beg You, don't torture me!" For Jesus had already said to the spirit, "Come out of the man, you evil spirit."

Then Jesus demanded, "What is your name?" And he replied, "My name is Legion, because there are many of us inside this man." Then the evil spirits begged him again and again not to send them to some distant place.

There happened to be a large herd of pigs feeding on the hillside nearby. "Send us into those pigs," the spirits begged. "Let us enter them."

So Jesus gave them permission. The evil spirits came out of the man and entered the pigs, and the entire herd of 2,000 pigs plunged down the steep hillside into the lake and drowned in the water.

The herdsmen fled to the nearby town and the surrounding countryside, spreading the news as they ran. People rushed out to see what had happened. A crowd soon gathered

*around Jesus, and they saw the man who had been pos-
sessed by the legion of demons. He was sitting there fully
clothed and perfectly sane, and they were all afraid. Then
those who had seen what happened told the others about the
demon-possessed man and the pigs. And the crowd began
pleading with Jesus to go away and leave them alone.*

*As Jesus was getting into the boat, the man who had been de-
mon possessed begged to go with Him. But Jesus said, "No,
go home to your family, and tell them everything the Lord has
done for you and how merciful He has been." So the man
started off to visit the Ten Towns of that region and began to
proclaim the great things Jesus had done for him; and everyone was amazed at what he told them* (Mark 5:1-20 NLT)

The Gospel of Mark also recounts how Jesus healed a little
girl who was demon possessed because her mother honored Jesus
and had faith in Christ to heal:

*Jesus left that place and went to the vicinity of Tyre. He
entered a house and did not want anyone to know it; yet
He could not keep His presence secret. In fact, as soon as
she heard about Him, a woman whose little daughter was
possessed by an evil spirit came and fell at His feet. The
woman was a Greek, born in Syrian Phoenicia. She begged
Jesus to drive the demon out of her daughter.*

*"First let the children eat all they want," He told her, "for it is
not right to take the children's bread and toss it to their dogs."*

*"Yes, Lord," she replied, "but even the dogs under the table
eat the children's crumbs."*

*Then He told her, "For such a reply, you may go; the de-
mon has left your daughter."*

She went home and found her child lying on the bed, and the demon gone (Mark 7:24-30).

Delivering people from the torment of demons was a large part of Jesus' ministry here on earth:

Jesus went throughout Galilee, teaching in their synagogues, preaching the good news of the kingdom, and healing every disease and sickness among the people. News about Him spread all over Syria, and people brought to Him all who were ill with various diseases, those suffering severe pain, the demon-possessed, those having seizures, and the paralyzed, and He healed them. Large crowds from Galilee, the Decapolis, Jerusalem, Judea and the region across the Jordan followed Him (Matthew 4:23-25)

In Acts, we learn that Jesus' ministry has been passed on to future generations. Paul was able to cast out demons by using the power of Jesus' name:

Once when we were going to the place of prayer, we were met by a slave girl who had a spirit by which she predicted the future. She earned a great deal of money for her owners by fortune-telling. This girl followed Paul and the rest of us, shouting, "These men are servants of the Most High God, who are telling you the way to be saved." She kept this up for many days. Finally Paul became so troubled that he turned around and said to the spirit, "In the name of Jesus Christ I command you to come out of her!" At that moment the spirit left her (Acts 16:16-18).

Demonic Strategies

As you can see from these biblical accounts, demons can and do torment people. Demons come to steal, kill, and destroy. The apostle Paul tells us to learn the enemy's schemes (see 2 Cor. 2:11) so we can counter satanic activity. The following strategies are employed by demons to achieve their goals:

1. *Making bad things worse:* We know that life's misfortunes are not always caused by demons. Still, Peter and Paul warned us to be alert in First Peter 5:8. The enemy is an opportunist. Negative circumstances often open doors of unforgiveness, bitterness, and the like. Satan can then make a mountain out of a molehill.

2. *Encouraging disruption:* Demons have limited ability to cause trouble. However, they push, prod, tempt, and entice people to live in rebellion, which leads to a host of trouble. In Luke 4:33, demons manifested in an attempt to disrupt the purposes of God.

3. *Using Temptation:* In Genesis 3, satan tempted Adam and Eve. Temptation led to their rebellion and the beginning of the sinful nature of humankind.

4. *Instilling Fear:* Fear is used by the enemy to prevent people from becoming fully aware of their authority as children of God. God has defeated satan. Therefore, he can only gain authority by tricking us or stealing what is not his. He knows that if we do not resist him, he is not required to flee (see James 4:7). Sir Edmund Burke, a British nobleman, once said, "A sure way for evil to triumph is for good men to do nothing." Many people fear the power in the demonic realm so they do nothing—they do not resist the devil.

But Paul told Timothy (see 2 Tim. 1:7) that God has not given us a spirit of fear, but of power, love, and a sound mind. If God has not given us fear, who has? The adversary has. Fear is rooted in doubt, disbelief and deception, none of which is from our Lord.

5. *Lying and Deceiving:* The father of lies is satan (see John 8:44). He can hinder unbelievers from believing in God (see 2 Cor. 4:4).

Clues to Demonic Involvement

By observing the fruit of a person's life and relationships, one can often discover clues to demonic influences. The following are the negative fruit that may indicate demonic involvement:

1. *Emotional:* Resentment, hatred, anger, fear, rejection, self-pity, jealousy, depression, worry, insecurity, anxiety, etc.

2. *Mental:* Disturbances in the mind or thought processes such as: torment, confusion, loss of memory, compromise, unbelief, indecision, or voices being heard.

3. *Speech:* Uncontrolled tongue, lying, cursing, criticism, gossip, mockery, or blasphemy.

4. *Sexual:* Recurring unclean thoughts or actions, fantasy, lust, perversion, homosexuality, adultery, fornication, incest, and seduction.

5. *Addictions:* Drugs, alcohol, food, nicotine, and compulsive behaviors.

6. *Physical Infirmities:* Many physical afflictions are a result of spirits of infirmity.

> *On a Sabbath Jesus was teaching in one of the synagogues, and a woman was there who had been crippled by a spirit for eighteen years. She was bent over and could not straighten up at all. When Jesus saw her, He called her forward and*

said to her, "Woman, you are set free from your infirmity." Then He put His hands on her, and immediately she
straightened up and praised God (Luke 13:10-13).

7. *Religious Error:* False religion, cults, the occult, spiritualism,
New Age, and false doctrines.

*The Spirit clearly says that in later times some will aban-
don the faith and follow deceiving spirits and things taught
by demons. Such teachings come through hypocritical liars, whose consciences have been seared as with a hot iron.
They forbid people to marry and order them to abstain from
certain foods, which God created to be received with thanksgiving by those who believe and who know the truth. For
everything God created is good, and nothing is to be rejected
if it is received with thanksgiving* (1 Timothy 4:1-4).

*...do not let your people practice fortune-telling, or use sor-
cery, or interpret omens, or engage in witchcraft, or cast
spells, or function as mediums or psychics, or call forth the
spirits of the dead. Anyone who does these things is detestable to the Lord. It is because the other nations have done
these detestable things that the Lord your God will drive them
out ahead of you. But you must be blameless before the Lord
your God. The nations you are about to displace consult
sorcerers and fortune-tellers, but the Lord your God forbids
you to do such things* (Deuteronomy 18:10-14 NLT).

Not all unrighteous or evil behavior can be attributed to demonic influence or presence. Humanity's heart and sinful nature
are sufficient to result in a lack of the fruit of the Holy Spirit.
If a person remains in sin or practices sin, the demonic realm is
attracted to this. Sinful nature can become the doorway to the

demonic. Discernment is essential to know when deliverance is warranted.

Discernment

You should not rely solely upon your observational skills, because not all negative behaviors are caused by demons. Moreover, demonic activity is frequently disguised or covered to avoid obvious detection.

If a demonic presence can remain hidden until the maximum damage can be done to the Body of Christ, satan gains an advantage. For this reason, I believe that every Christian should participate in prayer ministry. We all have past "baggage." I especially recommend that all leaders and ministry leaders participate in several prayer ministry sessions.

When a demonic presence fears being exposed, it will often go into hiding or start "behaving" to gain a strategic advantage. If this is not working, and the demonic presence is being pressured by the power of the Holy Spirit, the demon will often manifest in order to divert attention, make bold statements and lies, or do really dumb things to incriminate it. For example, high praise and worship may cause sickness, pain, blacking out, a strong desire to run, impure sexual thoughts, or even self-destructive or depressive thoughts.

The closer we get to the truth, to Jesus, and the more we seek forgiveness and repentance, the weaker the influence of darkness becomes in our lives. *The truth will set us free. Whom the Son sets free is free indeed!* (See John 8:32, Phil. 4:8, and John 14:17.)

The Word tells us in First Corinthians 12:10 that the ability to discern spirits is one of the supernatural gifts from the Holy Spirit. Learning to trust this inner knowing of the Spirit is very important as we battle to resist the enemy. During prayer min-istry sessions, we always ask the Holy Spirit to release the gifts needed in order to help facilitate the process of freedom.

As you can see from the experiences I have shared with you, demons are real and are aggressively seeking to influence people in negative ways. Fortunately, as you have seen in Part I, the abil-ity to cast out demons in Jesus' name is alive and well today. We simply need to raise up more servants of God to claim their au-thority in Jesus and to begin to deliver the multitude of tormented people in our generation.

Understand Your Authority

When engaging in prayer ministry, you must be aware of your identity as a child of God. With that knowledge, you should re-main confident in your authority to cast out demons. The enemy may try to deceive you by having you question your authority. Such doubts may instill fear and cause you to retreat. This is a primary tactic used by demons to maintain and occupy territory that has already been purchased by Jesus at the resurrection. Don't fall for such lies.

Remember that in John 14 we are told that we will do what Jesus did and accomplish even greater results. To gain confidence in your spiritual authority, read Luke 10:17-19 where Jesus made it clear that He has delegated His spiritual authority to all believers, including you:

> *The seventy-two returned with joy and said, "Lord, even the demons submit to us in Your name." He replied, "I saw Satan fall like lightning from heaven. I have given you authority to trample on snakes and scorpions and to overcome all the power of the enemy; nothing will harm you (Luke 10:17-19).*

As discussed previously, fear is another enemy tactic. An evil spirit may even threaten to kill the individual or the ministry team. Recall my real-life account of the demon that threatened to kill Mark during prayer ministry.

It is important to recognize that deception is satan's native tongue. After all, he is the father of lies (see John 8:44). Therefore, it is not surprising that all evil spirits are liars and deceivers. Remember your authority and power in Jesus and that God has not given you a spirit of fear, but of power, love, and a sound mind (see 2 Tim. 1:7). Then, with confidence and authority, cast that lying demon out in Jesus' name.

The Gospel of Mark describes Jesus' disappointment in His disciples because He had given them authority and they did not exercise it:

> *When they came to the other disciples, they saw a large crowd around them and the teachers of the law arguing with them. As soon as all the people saw Jesus, they were overwhelmed with wonder and ran to greet Him.*
>
> *"What are you arguing with them about?" He asked.*
>
> *A man in the crowd answered, "Teacher, I brought You my son, who is possessed by a spirit that has robbed him of speech. Whenever it seizes him, it throws him to the ground. He foams at the mouth, gnashes his teeth and becomes rigid. I asked Your disciples to drive out the spirit, but they could not."*
>
> *"O unbelieving generation," Jesus replied, "how long shall I stay with you? How long shall I put up with you? Bring the boy to Me"* (Mark 9:14-19).

Jesus then commanded the evil spirit to come out of the boy and healed the boy Himself. In this passage Jesus reveals His expectation that our faith be demonstrated by casting out dark-ness. He wants us to be aware of and demonstrate our authority.

Finally, be strong in the Lord and in His mighty power. Put on the full armor of God so that you can take your stand against the devil's schemes (Ephesians 6:10-11).

Submit yourselves, then, to God. Resist the devil, and he will flee from you (James 4:7).

Remember, the Lord would not tell us to resist and take a stand against the enemy without granting us the ability to be victorious.

CHAPTER 9

Beware of Strongholds

Demons are evil personalities. They are spirit beings. They are enemies of humanity that will torment, afflict, confuse, accuse, pressure, resist, and deceive. Demons gain access through open doors. They have to be given an opportunity or authorization for access. When the door has been opened and the enemy has gained access, he then has authorization to kill, steal, and destroy. In other words, the enemy has gained a stronghold.

Open doors can come from:

1. *Sin*: generational sin or sins of omission and commission

2. *Invitation*: conscious or unconscious

   - trauma or life's circumstances

   - believed lies

- places and objects

3. *Curses:* we accept or fail to rebuke

Sin

Remember that sinful behaviors are not always caused by demons, but the behavior can open the door to demonic influence. Sin can be caused by the individual or may be passed down from ancestors. The latter is known as generational sin. Sin can be summed up as falling short of God's perfect will for our lives. Sin will take you where you do not want to go. Sin will make you stay longer than you want to stay. Sin will make you pay more than you want to pay.

The following are examples of common behaviors that are seen as sin in the Bible:

- Rebellion is as the sin of witchcraft, and

- Stubbornness is as the sin of idolatry (see 1 Sam. 15:23).

- Righteousness, abstaining from sin, on the other hand, confers protection from demonization (see 2 Cor. 6:7)

Invitation

Demonization may occur through an unconscious or conscious invitation. A conscious invitation is a choice, like joining an organization like Free Masonry, attending séances, or visiting spiritualists. Unconscious invitation occurs when we wallow in negative attitudes resulting from difficult experiences. Remember, demons must have a legal right to gain access.

Paul instructed us not to give the devil a chance when we are angry (see Eph. 4:26-27). Wallowing in unconfessed sin is what John Wimber (founder of the Vineyard Association) once described as a runway with lights that illuminates the way for demons to land.[1]

Someone who has authority over another individual, such as a young child, can empower the demonic by providing an open door. For example, a parent may take a child to a spiritualist, which can invite demons to enter the child. The parent may be unaware of the consequences of their actions.

Children can also become demonized by generational or bloodline spiritual power.

> *You must not bow down to them or worship them, for I, the Lord your God, am a jealous God, who will not tolerate your affection for any other gods! I lay the sins of the parents upon their children; the entire family is affected—even children in the third and fourth generations…*(Exodus 20:5-6).

For instance, parents and grandparents who practice Freemasonry curse themselves and their family by swearing secret oaths.[2]

Curses

Although curses are another means of opening a door, cursing does not always result in demonization. Recall that righteousness serves as our protection. Curses cannot hurt you unless you deserve them. *"Like a fluttering sparrow or a darting swallow, an undeserved curse does not come to rest"* (Prov. 26:2 NIV). However, if a door eventually opens, a curse expedites the presence of darkness.

Trisha's Testimony

The following occurred while I was with a ministry team in Manchester, England, on a mission's outreach with Global Awakening.

During one of our meetings a woman, I will call her Trisha, came up to me for prayer. I discerned a spirit of death the moment I saw her. I asked her how I could pray for her and she told me about her fight with breast cancer. She had recently undergone a mastectomy and chemotherapy, yet ultimately she had lost her battle with breast cancer. As soon as I began to pray for her, she manifested by becoming stiff with her hands curled up. I immediately prayed for peace and her body relaxed. I asked her if she would be willing to come back the next day so we could spend focused time on her in a quiet setting. She agreed. I asked her to prepare for the ministry session by making a forgiveness and confession list.

The following day, my mother and prayer warrior, Marion Hauser, joined me along with two members from my church, Karen Baumen and Charles George. We quickly learned the following about open doors and curses that result in demonization.

Trisha had been a Christian for more than ten years and was active in church ministry. She went on to give us insight into her turbulent childhood. She indicated that she never felt any love from her mother growing up. Sadly, her older brother and an older man who babysat her as a child molested her. Although her first child had been born out of wedlock, she was currently married to the father of her three subsequent children.

She described an event four years prior to our meeting when she was asked to lead the Scripture reading for a Christmas Eve service. During the reading, she began to feel sick, and the sick feeling persisted to the next day when she discovered an unraveled cassette tape wrapped around some bushes at her house.

She explained that the witch covens regularly curse Christians by speaking curses into a tape recorder and then stringing the tape around churches or peoples' homes. Trisha believed the witches visited her home while she was attending the Christmas Eve service. After finding the tape, she simply picked it up and threw it away. Since then the following situations had occurred in her life:

1. All four of her children had been arrested.

2. She developed breast cancer.

3. Her husband quit attending church and began visiting a prostitute.

4. She had an affair while on vacation in Turkey.

5. She was asked to leave her church. As a result, she felt unloved by God and unable to worship anymore.

Trisha described her affair in Turkey in detail. She said that her mother initiated the event and expressed that the affair was justified by Trisha's husband's extracurricular activities. Her mother encouraged the date by purchasing a gold bracelet for Trisha, which she had continued to wear since the affair. Interestingly, the wrist she wore the bracelet on developed warts that no medication could eradicate. During the meeting there was a "word" given regarding a cursed piece of jewelry. So she immediately disposed of the bracelet in a church bathroom. Soon afterward, the warts miraculously disappeared.

During four hours of prayer ministry, using the Destiny Model of forgiveness and confession, we cast out spirits of rejection, selfishness, witchcraft, and death. During a manifestation, a demon spoke, "I don't have to leave!" I then commanded the spirit to tell us why it didn't have to leave. The spirit replied, "She is used to me." Trisha then motioned as if to strangle me. The spirit said, "I am going to get you!" I rebuked the spirit and informed it that it had no authority and it could not hurt me, Trisha, or any of the team members. I informed it that it had to leave!

Trisha began coughing a lot. We then seemed to hit a roadblock. We asked the Holy Spirit for divine insight. Team member Karen Bauman suddenly developed sharp pains in her stomach. Charles George quickly received a word of knowledge and asked Trisha if she had ever had an abortion. She replied yes and then confessed and repented of the murdering spirit. Charles then asked her if she had any sexual fantasies. She agreed and confessed this as well. After her confessions, I took authority over all unclean spirits and commanded them to leave her. The spirit then spoke again, "All right, I'll go." Immediately, Trisha became bright and clear-headed, declaring, "I'm free!"

Finally, we prayed for her to be filled with the Holy Spirit, placed the full armor of the Lord on her, and spoke a Mother and Father's Blessing[3] over her. She was filled with such joy. Together we raised our hands. She was ecstatic because she had previously been unable to raise her hands above her shoulders. Her shoulders were instantly healed! God is awesome!

ENDNOTES

1. The late John Wimber, founder of the Vineyard Association, said this at a conference.

2. See *The Deadly Deception* by James D. Shaw and Tom C. McKenney (Lafayette, LA: Vital Issues Press, 1988).

3. In the Old Testament, the Jewish patriarchs often blessed their children. See Genesis 27:4 and Genesis 48:15.

CHAPTER 10

Deal With Curses

What Is a Curse?

A curse is a prayer or invocation for harm, injury, or an evil fate to come upon a person. It may also be a pronouncement of doom or vengeance. People who minister to those under a curse add that a curse has a spiritual, demonic power to work evil.

The term curse does not always mean the utterance of the curse itself but the harm or injury that follows the utterance. For instance, when a series of unfavorable or disastrous circumstances occur, the affected person may be described as "under a curse."

How Curses Are Generated

It will help us deal with curses if we understand how they are generated. These are the most common:

1. Written or oral decrees

2. Careless statements

3. Involvement with a secret society or an occult activity or organization

4. Conduct that brings a curse upon the performer

5. The iniquities of ancestors that are passed on to descendants[1]

A curse is commonly thought of as something intended by one person to have a significant evil effect on another person. For instance, a person with a grievance against another may curse the other, or may engage a witch or witch doctor to place a hex on the other. In some cultures, it is common to ask a witch doctor to curse an enemy (see Num. 22:6-7).

Someone may curse another in the heat of rage or hate. Persons or families involved in violent quarrels, especially if protracted, may curse each other. Some cultures are known for the placement of intentional curses on families or clans. Scottish clans and Arab families, for example, and families in some sections of the United States and Africa, have historically engaged in vicious cycles of attack and retaliation against each other, frequently invoking curses upon each other.

The spread of satanic activities in North America has brought increased awareness of the practice of imposing curses on Christians and others. Such organizations also frequently have occult practices that can result in curses, such as vows of various kinds, contracts with satan or with other members, marrying satan, and so on.

A curse can be passed on from one generation to the next. Curses from occult practices tend to be generational. In fact, some illnesses and addictions that run in families may be caused by a curse. The prophet Elisha placed a generational curse of leprosy on Gehazi for his greed and dishonesty, *"Because you have done this, you and your descendants will suffer from Naaman's leprosy forever"* (2 Kings 5:27 NLT).

These examples are intentional curses, where the person invoking the curse knows what he is doing and intends to place a curse upon his target. However, a curse can also be unintentional or even self-imposed. These are often the result of careless speech. We need to guard our mouths from careless statements.

Death and life are in the power of the tongue... (Proverbs 18:21 NKJV).

An unintentional curse can result from careless words spoken by a parent, in exasperation or frustration, about the inability of a child to understand something or to perform an act to the parent's satisfaction. Such careless words may actually be curses affecting the future of the child:

- "You can't do anything right."

- "You'll never amount to anything."

- "You are just plain dumb."

- "You'll never be able to hold a job."

- "You'll probably be sick all your life."

- "You'll have heart trouble like your father."

A wholesome tongue is a tree of life, but perverseness in it breaks the spirit (Proverbs 15:4 NKJV).

Such pronouncements can sink into a person's mind and become a spiritual bondage—a demonic bondage—resulting in exactly the condition described by the parent. This type of curse can be placed on a person by anyone in authority, such as a teacher, military officer, employer, or parent.

Unintended curses can also be self-imposed by careless words. Some examples:

- "She drives me crazy."

- "I get sick every time I think of that."

- "I would like to die."

- "I'm scared to death of…"

- "I'm embarrassed to death."

- "Cross my heart and hope to die…"

A somewhat different kind of curse can be self-imposed by a person who is so deeply offended by someone else's conduct that he vows never to engage in such conduct. A child may be so offended by a parent's conduct—for example, controlling the household by going into rages over small things—that the child vows inwardly never to engage in the offensive conduct. Such vows can sometimes create demonic bondage that the child cannot overcome, and he finds himself engaging in the same conduct that offended him so much in his parent.

Certain types of conduct may bring forth curses. Such conduct often has a spiritual dimension, such as participating in the occult practices of a satanic cult, or disobeying a command of God.

Mere participation in some activities, such as satanic cults and Freemasonry, can have significant adverse effects on a person and on his or her family. For example, the extended families of Freemasons frequently exhibit what seems to be the effect of a curse, such as unusual numbers of divorces, incurable illnesses, addictions, accidents, and premature deaths. Sometimes an activity by a Freemason seems to have an effect on a family member.

For example, one particular Masonic ritual involves placing a noose around the member's neck. A member of the family of such a member had difficulty breathing until the apparent curse related to that noose was broken.

There are a number of passages in the Bible that deal with curses placed upon a person or group because of the conduct of the person or group. Deuteronomy 27 details a number of types of conduct that can result in curses, either for an individual or for a group.

"Cursed is the man who carves an image or casts an idol— a thing detestable to the Lord, the work of the craftsman's hands—and sets it up in secret." Then all the people shall say, "Amen!"

"Cursed is the man who dishonors his father or his mother." Then all the people shall say, "Amen!"

"Cursed is the man who moves his neighbor's boundary stone." Then all the people shall say, "Amen!"

"Cursed is the man who leads the blind astray on the road." Then all the people shall say, "Amen!"

"Cursed is the man who withholds justice from the alien, the fatherless or the widow." Then all the people shall say, "Amen!"

"Cursed is the man who sleeps with his father's wife, for he dishonors his father's bed." Then all the people shall say, "Amen!"

"Cursed is the man who has sexual relations with any animal." Then all the people shall say, "Amen!"

"Cursed is the man who sleeps with his sister, the daughter of his father or the daughter of his mother." Then all the people shall say, "Amen!"

"Cursed is the man who sleeps with his mother-in-law." Then all the people shall say, "Amen!"

"Cursed is the man who kills his neighbor secretly." Then all the people shall say, "Amen!"

"Cursed is the man who accepts a bribe to kill an innocent person." Then all the people shall say, "Amen!"

"Cursed is the man who does not uphold the words of this law by carrying them out." Then all the people shall say, "Amen!" (Deuteronomy 27:15-26).

Types of Curses

A curse can result in general misfortune or it can be intended to result specifically in any one or more of a long list of unfortunate conditions or disasters such as sickness, barrenness, social or economic misfortune, susceptibility to accidents, fears, torment, and death.

A curse can be conditional or unconditional. A conditional curse is intended to take effect only if a prerequisite is met. An example of a conditional curse is the invocation of terrible physical harm if a member of a Masonic lodge or satanic cult breaks its rules of secrecy. Those who make these vows of secrecy presume that if they are careful to observe their vows, the curses will not fall upon them.

Conditional Curses

Many examples of conditional curses can be found in the Old Testament. One example is the curse that the Lord indicated He would impose on the Israelites for disobeying His commands, *"Cursed is the man who does not uphold the words of this law by carrying them out"* (Deut. 27:26).

Conditional curses also occur in the New Testament:

When the Son of Man comes in His glory, and all the holy angels with Him, then He will sit on the throne of His glory. All the nations will be gathered before Him, and He will separate them one from another, as a shepherd divides his sheep from the goats. And He will set the sheep on His right hand, but the goats on the left (Matthew 25:31-33 NKJV).

Then He will also say to those on the left hand, 'Depart from Me, you cursed, into the everlasting fire prepared for the devil and his angels: for I was hungry and you gave Me no food; I was thirsty and you gave Me no drink; I was a stranger and you did not take Me in; naked and you did not clothe Me; sick and in prison and you did not visit Me. … inasmuch as you did not do it to one of the least of these, you did not do it to Me.' And these will go away into everlasting punishment… (Matthew 25:41-43, 45-46 NKJV).

Unconditional Curses

Examples of unconditional curses are those imposed by a witch or a witch doctor that are intended to impose illness, disaster, death, or harm upon an enemy of the witch's or witch doctor's client. These are intended to operate irrespective of the circumstances.

A New Testament example of an unconditional curse—this one self-imposed—is that of the Jewish crowd who filled Pilate's courtyard with cries for the crucifixion of Jesus. When Pilate washed his hands and declared he was innocent of the blood of Jesus, those present who were clamoring for Jesus to be crucified cried out, *"His blood be on us and on our children"* (Matt. 27:25).

The Effects of Curses

As noted, a curse typically has spiritual power. It can, and often does, have the effect intended by the one who invokes it, and it may have other effects, as well. The curse's spiritual power is not derived from God, but from satan.

In *Healing Through Deliverance: The Practical Ministry*, Peter Horrobin defines a curse as "something said or done against us or others which gives rights to the demonic to exercise power over people."[2]

Unbroken curses often have consequences other than their intended effects. For example, curses may impede or prevent healing or deliverance. They may also cause a general malaise resulting in poor health, lack of success in one's occupation, financial problems, family difficulties, and so on.

A conditional curse can also have negative effects not related to the stated condition of the curse. Membership in a secret society or in a satanic cult can instill a curse of its own upon the person involved or his family, even if the person involved faithfully performs all his promised duties. Even if the member of the organization is faithful to his vows, the demonic nature of his activity can, and often does, give rise to a curse.

Curses can be placed on objects resulting in general malaise in a house or other place. Such curses can be induced by a demonic icon, which may exist as demonic symbols in tapestries, china, or other decorations; totem poles; hideous statuettes; distorted images; things that have been worshiped; and false gods, temples of false gods, idols, cursed objects, jewelry, or symbols.

Seek discernment and the Holy Spirit will make you aware of the presence of evil in certain places. This can be discerned by odors, uneasiness, sickness, or heaviness. All these may be signs from the Holy Spirit to be on guard. So be aware! Hebrews 5:14 states: those by reason of use have their senses exercised to discern both good and evil (KJV).

How to Recognize the Presence of a Curse

Curses can often be recognized when the person is being interviewed in preparation for prayer ministry. A curse may be discovered in the following ways:

- The person receiving ministry knows he has been cursed and can identify the person who placed the curse on him, when it happened, and the type of curse. For example, if a curse was invoked in the course of a violent quarrel, the person may remember it.

- The person who placed the curse or procured it may tell the cursed person in order to torment him.

- A person or a family member may have had involvement in occult practices, rituals, organizations, or satanic contracts. Such involvement is a common origin point for curses.

- Membership in a secret society such as a Masonic organization is an indication that a curse may be present.

- Difficult relationships with various authority figures (parents, teachers, military officers, police, employers, etc.) in the person's life. An authority figure may have spoken unintentional curses into his life through derogatory statements.

- The person receiving ministry may have imposed curses upon themselves. Curses may be identified by self-deprecating statements.

Certain conditions should lead us to suspect that a curse is present, even if none of the previous clues are present. Derek Prince lists the following as likely indications of a curse when two or more are present:

- Mental or emotional breakdown

- Repeated or chronic sickness, especially if hereditary

- Barrenness, a tendency to miscarry; mental problems

- Breakdown of marriage and family alienation

- Continuing financial insufficiency

- Accident proneness

- A family history of suicides, early deaths or unnatural deaths[3]

Once prayer ministry is begun, the following are additional clues that are suggestive of the presence of a curse:

- Difficulty receiving prayer for the presence of the Holy Spirit

- Lack of progress when praying for healing

- If there seems to be a "wall" when praying for a person

How to Break a Curse

Because it has demonic power, the bondage of a curse lasts indefinitely, unless broken. When a curse is present, it often must be dealt with before a successful prayer for healing or deliverance can take place.

The power and authority to break curses comes from Jesus. Jesus' blood, which was shed on the cross, released the forgiveness of sin as well as the power for healing, deliverance, and to break curses. In his letter to the Galatians, Paul observed:

> *Christ has redeemed us from the curse of the law, having become a curse for us (for it is written, "Cursed is everyone who is hanged on a tree"), that the blessing of Abraham might come upon the gentiles in Christ Jesus, that we might receive the promise of the Spirit through faith* (Galatians 3:13-14 NKJV).

Breaking the bondage of a curse often requires ministry by another person or team of people. A curse can, however, be broken in the name of Jesus by the person who is under it.

People who have been cursed are most likely to get relief if they have prepared themselves spiritually in the following manner:

1. Repented of all rebellion and sin in their life

2. Asked for and claimed forgiveness for all their sins

3. Forgiven everyone who has injured them

4. Renounced all contact with anything occultic or satanic

Once this spiritual preparatory work has been completed, one can pray all curses would be broken and inner wounds caused by these curses would be healed. By faith, a person can receive what they have asked for.

It may be evident that a specific statement made by an authority figure has festered in a person's mind and spirit, such as a statement by a father that his son would "never amount to anything." Reciting the following prayer can break such a curse:

> In the name of Jesus, I break the curse over Joe's life resulting from his father's statements that Joe would never amount to anything. I break the power of those words over Joe, in the name of Jesus. In the name of Jesus, I break any bondage of those words over Joe.

This should be followed by prayer for healing of any damage to Joe's spirit or emotions caused by the derogatory words spoken to him.

A similar prayer can be made in the case of a witch's hex or other known imprecation, specifically mentioning each separate curse that was pronounced.

Often a father or other authority figure may have given way to exasperation or exaggeration, and may have made *many* derogatory statements about the person receiving ministry—too many to remember. When details cannot be remembered, a more general prayer is appropriate, such as:

> In the name of Jesus, I break every curse on Joe resulting from his father's careless statements about his lack of ability, his lack of intelligence, and his limited future possibilities. I break their power over Joe in the name of Jesus. In the name of Jesus, I break the bondage of any such words

*over Joe's life. In the name of Jesus, I pray for the healing
of all wounds in Joe resulting from these curses.*

If other people made such statements, such as a teacher, military officer, close friend, and so on, the power of those statements should also be broken in the name of Jesus.

Note: It is important to remember that the person who is reciting the prayer is *not* the one who is breaking the curse. *Only Jesus can do this.* The prayer is simply a means to summon Jesus' power and authority.

In cases involving a careless statement or satanic contract that a person said or made about his or her own life, the person should go through the preparatory steps mentioned previously and then address the following additional items:

1. The careless statement must be renounced.

2. Any vow not to engage in certain conduct must be renounced.

3. Any vow to the secret society or satanic society must be renounced.

4. The curse pronounced on oneself must be renounced.

5. The satanic vow and contract must be renounced.

6. Membership in the secret society or in the occult organization must be renounced.

7. If ancestral iniquity is involved, it must be repented of.

Remember that each step should be taken in the name of Jesus. For example, "In Jesus' name, I renounce my vow never to be like my mother."

Then the person under the curse must repent of his own conduct and ask and receive the Lord's forgiveness. After this, the power of the curse can be broken in the name of Jesus.

The person freed from the curse should destroy any mementos or symbols in his possession of the society or cult or activity that caused the curse, such as jewelry (rings, earrings, cufflinks, bracelets, etc.), paper weights, plaques, certificates, uniforms, T-shirts, and so on.

Tokens or symbols of the occult activity, if retained, can continue to have an oppressive, demonic power over the person, and even over others living or working in the same environment.

Occult activity and membership in occult organizations, such as the Masons, can affect family members who have had no contact with the organization on their own. Such family members should renounce the organization, renounce any vows or contracts made by ancestors or relatives, and then the curse should be broken in the name of Jesus.[4]

For members of the family of a Freemason, a renunciation and prayer along the following lines should suffice:

In the name of Jesus, I renounce every oath taken and the curses and the related penalties pronounced by any ancestor or other relative of mine in any ritual of Freemasonry. I renounce every god honored and every password used in any degree, and every spirit causing any illness or disease, in the name of Jesus. I renounce every death wish and every symbolic ritual, such as burial and resurrection, in the name of Jesus. Father, I ask You to wash me clean of all uncleanliness connected with Freemasonry, and to free me from any bondage to fear or any emotional or occultic influence from

Freemasonry. In the name of Jesus, I break the power over me of any unclean spirit related to Freemasonry.[5]

If the person receiving ministry can remember particular oaths or curses that seem to have an untoward effect on him, they should be added to the list of those renounced and broken.

As noted, some curses flow from one generation to the next. Often family members are afflicted with the same problems that their ancestors had, such as proneness to illness, accidents, poverty, or addiction. These generational ties can be broken by the person ministering, or by the person receiving ministry, by a prayer in the name of Jesus.

Love your enemies, do good to those who hate you, bless those who curse you, and pray for those who spitefully use you (Luke 6:27-28 NKJV).

Bless those who persecute you; bless and do not curse (Romans 12:14).

If a believer has pronounced any curse, he must repent of this conduct and ask for God's forgiveness, as he would for any other sin. In addition, he or she should pronounce a blessing on the other person to replace the curse and pray for any necessary healing and restoration for the cursed one.

The believer should also be wary of unintended curses caused by careless remarks about another. These also should be repented of and a blessing substituted. If anyone feels these unintended curses are not important, he should consider these remarks of the Lord:

A good man out of the good treasure of his heart brings forth good things, and an evil man out of the evil treasure brings forth evil things. But I say to you that for every idle word men may speak, they will give account of it in the day of judgment. For by your words you will be justified, and by your words you will be condemned (Matthew 12:35-37 NKJV).

It is easy for some to fall into the habit of making derogatory statements about others, thereby placing unintended curses upon others. Special efforts should be made to break this habit.

What Is Freemasonry?

Randy Clark reveals the truth behind these secret societies in his Ministry Team Training Manual,[6] and Barbara Cassada discusses breaking the curses from our families in more detail in her book *Unto Death.*[7]

Freemasonry is sometimes viewed as a benevolent civic and social society, partly because of their organized fellowship and care for one another. Their most recognizable charitable organizations are the Shriners' hospitals, where needy children can obtain free medical care.

I believe, however, that Freemasonry is actually a deceptive religious organization that is blasphemous in its origin and practice.

The original concept of the Scottish Rite Freemasonry was to develop a universal religion that people of any faith could accept and worship in. Its buildings are called temples; they contain many religious items and symbols, including thrones, holy books, and altars. Its rituals combine elements of various religions, which are all considered equally godly. Masonic literature makes it clear that Freemasonry was founded and exists as a religion.

The Freemasonry "god" is a combination of Jehovah, Baal, and Osiris, though this is not disclosed to members until they are somewhat advanced in the society. The divinity of Jesus is denied. Freemasons believe that there is a war between lucifer and the Hebrew God, but lucifer is considered beneficent and the Hebrew God evil. Accordingly, Freemasonry is clearly occultic, blasphemous, and demonic.

There are devices in Freemasonry designed to make various Masonic rituals appear to be Christian. The Bible is accepted as a holy book—though only as one of several. Many prayers similar to those set out in the New Testament are used in rituals, though the name of Jesus is excised from all of them. A number of rituals use symbolism from the New Testament, such as symbolic death, burial, and resurrection. Since the true God is not worshiped or honored, these practices are deceptive.

Freemasonry seems to be particularly malignant in affecting the physical and emotional lives of members and their families. Members are required to pronounce upon themselves extremely vicious curses, such as dismemberment of their bodies in various hideous ways or death by various cruel means, as a penalty for violation of their secrecy vows. These truly sick curses vary in detail from one Masonic degree to another.

Former members or relatives of members do not often receive healing, deliverance, or the baptism in the Holy Spirit until the oaths, curses, and demonic rituals of Freemasonry are renounced and the curses are broken.

Janilda's Testimony

I was ministering at a facility for drug addicts and prostitutes in Madrid, Spain, in 2004. During the praise and worship portion of the service, a 14-year-old girl named Janilda fell to the floor and manifested. She was exhibiting tormenting behaviors, such as banging her head and pulling her hair. I, along with three team members, picked up the girl, with her mother's permission, and took her to a quiet room. Her mother served as our translator.

We took authority over the demonic spirits and spoke peace to the girl. I asked the mother if we could perform deliverance ministry on her daughter. She begged yes, as she was extremely distressed over her daughter's condition. The young girl, Janilda, was severely tormented and was often unable to speak. The mother indicated that the torment had been terrible for a long time.

Suspecting generational sin, I began by explaining generational sin and forgiveness to Janilda's mother. She began to weep while I was speaking to her. I took her aside and pressed her for the truth; but we hit a wall. The spirit tormenting Janilda was still strong and authorized to be present. Finally, the mother began to open up. She said that she had been a Christian for eight years. Janilda, however, had been born out of wedlock and her father, Janilda's grandfather, had forced her and her two sisters into prostitution.

Moreover, Janilda's grandmother was involved in witchcraft. Accordingly, the mother confessed, repented, and forgave her father, mother, and herself. This broke the authorization of the generational curse.

After I took authority, in Jesus' name, over witchcraft, prostitution, immorality, and rejection, the young woman became peaceful—but not totally free. Then I had Janilda confess Jesus as her Lord and Savior and renounce witchcraft, an orphan spirit, rejection, and abandonment. Subsequently, the demonic presence left. When she prayed to receive the Holy Spirit, it was glorious! She and her mother hugged and cried in each other's arms. Team member Phil Walls prayed the Father's blessing over her and gave her twenty dollars, as it was Janilda's spiritual birthday! She was a new creature in Christ Jesus, and we gave Him the victory!

ENDNOTES

1. Randy Clark, *Global Awakening Ministry Team Training Manual* (Pennsylvania: Apostolic Network of Global Awakening, 2011), L-4.

2. Peter Horrobin, *Healing Through Deliverance: the Practical Ministry* (Ada, MI: Chosen Books, 2003).

3. Derek Prince, *Blessing or Curse: You Can Choose* (Grand Rapids, MI: Chosen Books, 2006), 53.

4. Randy Clark, *Global Awakening Ministry Team Training Manual* (Pennsylvania: Apostolic Network of Global Awakening, 2011), L-11.

5. Barbara Cassada, *Unto Death* (Tome Publishing, 2007).

6. Randy Clark, *Global Awakening Ministry Team Training Manual* (Pennsylvania: Apostolic Network of Global Awakening, 2011), L-13.

7. Cassada, *Unto Death*.

CHAPTER 11

Dispel Myths

"And you will know the truth. And the truth will set you free" (John 8:32 NLT).

In Charles Kraft's book, *Defeating Dark Angels*, he lists 12 myths that are worth considering.[1] I have listed nine that I want to discuss. These myths are lies that provide strongholds in thinking or potential doorways that can hinder breaking free from darkness.

Myth #1: Christians Can't Be Demonized

Some argue that Christians cannot be possessed by demons. I agree because demons cannot inhabit the same space as God's Holy Spirit. Jesus sacrificed His life to remove our sins, which allows the Holy Spirit to reside in our spirits. This is what the terms "blood bought" or "His purchased possession" mean (see 1 Cor. 6:20).

However, a Christian can be under the power or influence of a demon. Our minds, wills, and emotions—the soul—and our flesh can be influenced by darkness; therefore, diligence is required on our part. This is the reason for Paul's advice in Galatians 5:

> So I say, live by the Spirit, and you will not gratify the desires of the sinful nature. For the sinful nature desires what is contrary to the Spirit, and the Spirit what is contrary to the sinful nature. They are in conflict with each other, so that you do not do what you want. But if you are led by the Spirit, you are not under the law.
>
> The acts of the sinful nature are obvious: sexual immorality, impurity and debauchery; idolatry and witchcraft; hatred, discord, jealousy, fits of rage, selfish ambition, dissensions, factions and envy; drunkenness, orgies, and the like. I warn you, as I did before, that those who live like this will not inherit the kingdom of God.
>
> But the fruit of the Spirit is love, joy, peace, patience, kindness, goodness, faithfulness, gentleness, and self-control. Against such things there is no law. Those who belong to Christ Jesus have crucified the sinful nature with its passions and desires. Since we live in the Spirit, let us keep in step with the Spirit. Let us not become conceited, provoking and envying each other (Galatians 5:16-26).

The Greek word *daimonizomai*, translated in the King James as possessed with devils, is more accurately translated to be "under the power of a demon."[2] Webster's dictionary defines possessed by demons as "affected by demons or invisible agents."

Frank Hammond, in his book *Demons and Deliverance*, describes demons as trespassers and Christians as the legal owner to the property.[3] Can property owned by one person be trespassed upon by another? Of course! But when a trespasser is confronted, and legal right is demonstrated, the trespasser will be required to leave because the law supports the owner. When an owner, or a delegated authority, confronts an evil spirit and commands it to leave—provided the demon's legal rights and authorization have been canceled—the demon then has no choice but to be evicted.

Myth #2: Deliverance Is Only Required Once

Dealing with spiritual and emotional hurts and lies requires time and process. Prayer ministry is a tool to wholeness and follow-up is best. Most people are like onions rather than bananas. Each layer has to be peeled back to get to the truth; and in most cases, this requires more than one session. The truth sets us free, but we can only bear a certain amount at a time (see John 16:12-13). Paul tells us, "That He [Jesus] who began a good work in you will carry it on to completion until the day of Jesus Christ" (Phil. 1:6). There are times in the Scriptures when deliverance and healing required prayer and process. At least three times it was not immediate: the situation with the Gerasene man when Jesus commanded demons to leave (see Mark 5:8); when He healed the blind man (see Mark 8:22-26); and when Jesus healed the demonized child and taught his disciples that some deliverances requires prayer and fasting (see Mark 9:29)

Myth #3: Demonization Is Simply Psychological

Not all psychological disturbances are a result of demonic influences. However, psychological problems can be caused by demons; and if this is the case, standard psychiatric treatment will not be effective. As I have seen from the fruit of experience, if a demonic influence is present, it must be cast out. Reliance on counseling and drugs will not get to the root of the problem. Demons, when present, must be cast out to obtain healing. At times, both medical and spiritual approaches need to work together for healing.

Myth #4: All Emotional Problems are Caused by Demons

Emotional problems are seldom caused by demons. We just can't simply assume that every problem is connected to a demon. Emotional hurt is one thing and demonic influence is another issue. If we first deal with the hurt and the lies, and then discover that demonic influence has been attracted, subsequent prayer ministry can help. The demonic presence can be cast out.

Myth #5: Problems are Either Demonic or Emotional

Problems can be either demonic or emotional, but they can also be a result of both. Demons are attracted to the sin, lies, and hurt that frequently result from emotional wounds. An emotional wound is usually the root of the problem. Healing this wound will generally lead to wholeness and emotional freedom. Resolving emotional wounds eliminates the garbage that attracts darkness and demons. Demons can be eradicated by deliverance once the garbage is gone, so they do not return.

Myth #6: Demonization in the United States is Uncommon

This assumption hinges on the belief that the Christian influence in America has been sufficient to hinder demonic influences in the U.S. However, due to the steady decline in morality in the U.S., there has been an increasing interest and intrigue in the occult, especially among youth. The popular Harry Potter books and movies evidence this. Shockingly, many public schools have made *Harry Potter* books mandatory reading. I believe that Deuteronomy 18:11-14 forbids this type of behavior and declares that those who participate in these practices are objects of horror and disgust to the Lord.

Nearly all American cities have a wide variety of occult establishments. In them, demonic power is used and passed on by people called palm readers, fortune-tellers, psychics, tarot card readers, spiritualists, scientologists, and so on. Accordingly, Masons, Christian Scientists, Buddhists, and Muslims are on the rise and opening people to demonic doctrines.

In *Time Magazine's* June 10, 1991 issue, an article describes the growing popularity of using non-orthodox medical and occult practices for healing. It also cites satanic rituals, and the horrific abuses that are associated with them, as a growing trend in America.

These practices and belief systems are directly correlated with demonization.[4]

Myth #7: Only Those With a Special Gifting Can Cast Out Demons

There are no special gifts for deliverance mentioned in the New Testament (see 1 Cor. 12:1-4; Rom. 12:1-8; Eph. 4:1-16; 1 Pet. 4:7-21). All believers have the authority and directive to go and to do as Jesus did (see Mark 16:15-18). Jesus made a serious declaration in the Great Commission: *"These miraculous signs will accompany those who believe. They will cast out demons in my name*" (Mark 16:17 NLT). If we believe in Jesus, then casting out demons is a sign that should follow us!

Myth #8: Inner Voices and Personality Switching Is Sure Evidence of Demonization

When a person is hearing voices, or seems to be under the control of something angry or hateful, we may assume that they are under the influence of demons. However, this is not always the case. While we have seen demons influence behavior and be responsible for voices, certain psychological conditions can also be responsible.

For example, a person with multiple personality disorder (MPD) is often also demonized. The demons, however, are not the root of the problem. According to James Friesen, "97 percent of MPD patients were victims of severe childhood abuse."[5] Therefore, casting out demons will not bring healing. These individuals require healing of their emotional wounds and re-integration of their personalities. People who suffer from multiple personality disorder have two or more distinct personalities, each of which is dominant at a particular time. Personalities are different from demons and need to be treated differently. Integrating multiple personalities back into one can be hindered if a personality is mistaken for a demon and cast out. Demons will often try to hinder integration with the core personality, as this will frequently result in healing.

A loving approach and listening for the Holy Spirit to guide us is very important in handling these situations. None of us have all the answers or the best approach, but the Lord Jesus sure does!

Myth #9: Anyone Can Receive Deliverance

Charles Kraft[6] does not list this myth, but I included it because I believe it is important.

Although it is true that anyone, believers and nonbelievers alike, *can* have demons cast out, this doesn't mean that nonbelievers *should* have demons cast out. In Matthew 15:26-28, Jesus refers to deliverance as "the children's bread" and not for those outside the covenant of God.

His likely reasoning for this is that the displaced demon can return with seven more demonic spirits. If the person has not filled himself with the Holy Spirit, the demons will have ample space to enter and cause more torment than before. Jesus warns of the necessity to fill the vacated home (the temple of the person), so the evil spirit doesn't return with seven demonic buddies to an unfilled house. Jesus said:

> *"When an evil spirit comes out of a man, it goes through arid places seeking rest and does not find it. Then it says, 'I will return to the house I left.' When it arrives, it finds the house unoccupied, swept clean and put in order. Then it goes and takes with it seven other spirits more wicked than itself, and they go in and live there. And the final condition of that man is worse than the first. That is how it will be with this wicked generation"* (Matthew 12:43-45).

Only believers can be filled by the Holy Spirit.

Prayer ministry and deliverance should be provided only to those who believe in Jesus Christ and want to be filled with the Holy Spirit. To do otherwise can often bring more torment to the individual. Only those who know Jesus Christ (believers) should perform deliverance. Acts 19:13-16 describes seven sons of Sceva who had a bad time doing deliverance. They were not believers and they were beaten and stripped naked. Now that's a bad day at the office!

ENDNOTES

1. Charles Kraft, *Defeating Dark Angels* (Ventura, CA: Regal Books, 1992).

2. See Thayer's *Greek-English Lexicon*.

3. Frank Hammond, *Demons and Deliverance* (Kirkwood, MO: Impact Christian Books, 2011).

4. For further information on this topic, I recommend reading *Uncovering the Mystery of Multiple Personality Disorder* by Dr. James G. Friesen.

5. James Friesen, *Uncovering the Mystery of Multiple Personality Disorder* (Eugene, OR: Wipf and Stock Publishing, 1997).

6. Charles Kraft, *Defeating Dark Angels* (Ventura, CA: Regal Books, 1992).

CHAPTER 12

Heal Yourself and Others

There are many approaches to healing yourself and others through the power of Jesus Christ. Most often, the techniques employed are labeled as "Prayer Ministry" or "Deliverance." Although the method may vary from church to church or person to person, the methodology should always be based upon Scripture.

The following steps are generally accepted as essential to effective healing through the power of Jesus Christ:

I. Ask the Holy Spirit to direct the session.

The Holy Spirit knows the truth that will set a person free. It is essential to ask Him and let Him lead the team. We are merely facilitators in the process.

But the Counselor, the Holy Spirit, whom the Father will send in My name, will teach you all things and will remind you of everything I have said to you (John 14:26).

There is so much more I want to tell you, but you can't bear it now. When the Spirit of truth comes, He will guide you into all truth. He will not speak on His own but will tell you what He has heard. He will tell you about the future (John 16:12-13 NLT).

And everyone who calls on the name of the Lord will be saved; for on Mount Zion and in Jerusalem there will be deliverance, as the Lord said, among the survivors whom the Lord calls (Joel 2:32).

I will instruct thee and teach thee in the way which thou shalt go: I will guide thee with mine eye (Psalm 32:8 KJV).

2. Forgive.

Forgiveness is absolutely essential in the ministry process, because unconfessed sin gives the devil a legal right to remain. It is important to note this is not about feelings; it is an act of our will.

Then Peter came to Jesus and asked, "Lord, how many times shall I forgive my brother when he sins against me? Up to seven times?"

Jesus answered, "I tell you, not seven times, but seventy-seven times. Therefore, the kingdom of heaven is like a king who wanted to settle accounts with his servants. As he began the settlement, a man who owed him ten thousand talents was brought to him. Since he was not able to pay, the master ordered that he and his wife and his children and all that he had be sold to repay the debt. The servant fell on his knees before him. 'Be patient with me,' he begged, 'and I will pay back everything.' The servant's master took pity on him, canceled the debt and let him go. But when that servant went out, he found one of his fellow servants who owed him a hundred denarii. He grabbed him and began to choke him. 'Pay back what you owe me!' he demanded. His fellow servant fell to his knees and begged him, 'Be patient with me, and I will pay you back.' But he refused. Instead, he went off and had the man thrown into prison until he could pay the debt. When the other servants saw what had happened, they were greatly distressed and went and told their master everything that had happened. Then the master called the servant in. 'You wicked servant,' he said, 'I canceled all that debt of yours because you begged me to. Shouldn't you have had mercy on your fellow servant just as I had on you?' In anger his master turned him over to the jailers to be tortured, until he should pay back all he owed. This is how My heavenly Father will treat each of you unless you forgive your brother from your heart" (Matthew 18:21-35).

If you forgive those who sin against you, your heavenly Father will forgive you. But if you refuse to forgive others, your Father will not forgive your sins (Mathew 6:14-15 NLT).

3. Renounce ungodly connections.

Ungodly connections transfer legal rights to the enemy. By renouncing, breaking, or severing any ungodly connections—including soul ties to unholy relationships and contracts or vows with darkness—one regains authority over his or her life. Destroying idols or symbols is a way to demonstrate repentance and will also unauthorize the legal rights the enemy once held. These strategies weaken the enemy's hold and influence.

Many who became believers confessed their sinful practices. A number of them who had been practicing magic brought their incantation books and burned them at a public bonfire. The value of the books was several million dollars (Acts 19:18-19 NLT).

4. Confront evil.

Jesus did not counsel demons, nor was He polite to them. He ordered them, and they obeyed. Whenever you are able, name the spirits specifically, address them in the authority of Jesus' name, and command them to leave the person. For example, you may say: "In the name of Jesus, I command you spirit of infirmity to leave this man." Some ministers prefer to ask Jesus to take authority and cast out demons Himself. An example of this approach is: "Jesus, this demon of infirmity has no legal rights over this man. I ask you to command this demon to leave." I don't believe this is the correct biblical approach. We have authority!

These miraculous signs will accompany those who believe: They will cast out demons in my name, and they will speak in new languages (Mark 16:17 NLT).

Look, I have given you authority over all the power of the enemy, and you can walk among snakes and scorpions and crush them. Nothing will injure you (Luke 10:19 NLT).

So humble yourselves before God. Resist the devil and he will flee from you (James 4:7 NLT).

The following qualities of the recipient are essential to the success of personal or corporate healing:

I. Truthfulness.

It is important for people who seek healing and deliverance to be truthful so that they may confess all of their sins, thereby weakening the enemy's power and authority over them.

Finally I confessed all my sins to You and stopped trying to hide my guilt. I said to myself, "I will confess my rebellion to the Lord." And You forgave me! All my guilt is gone" (Psalm 32:5 NLT).

Verbalize the following petition to God to help recall sins and transgressions that should be confessed:

Search me, O God, and know my heart; test me and know my anxious thoughts. Point out anything in me that offends you, and lead me along the path of everlasting life (Psalm 139:23-24 NLT).

2. Humility.

God will resist the proud and give grace to the humble. Pride and fear are tactics used by the enemy to prevent us from confessing our sins. Such sins are grounded in distrust and self-righteousness. Recall that we have *all* sinned and fallen short of God's glory. Fortunately, the blood of Jesus is more than enough to forgive our sin (see 1 John 1:9). All we have to do is confess our sins to Jesus; He is faithful to forgive us of all unrighteousness.

"God opposes the proud but gives grace to the humble." Submit yourselves, then, to God. Resist the devil, and he will flee from you (James 4:6b-7).

In addition to confessing our sins to God, prayer ministry has the additional benefit of allowing us the opportunity to confess our faults to other believers, which is powerful; it can destroy the lies we have believed—leading to healing of our minds and emotions. Confessing our faults to one another brings healing.

> *Confess your sins to each other and pray for each other so that you may be healed...* (James 5:16).

I have found that this is a very powerful part of the prayer ministry process:

- Confess your sins one to another that you may be healed. We are usually ok with confessing privately to Jesus, but confessing to others is humbling and requires trust and defying the fear of man.

- When two or three are gathered in His name, He is there. Let everything be established by two or three witnesses. Ganging up on the devil is biblical. He sent them out in twos (see Luke 9-10).

- Jesus and Paul taught that there were different kinds of demons and levels of evil that go out by prayer and fasting (see Mark 9:29; Eph. 6:10-18).

Moreover, if two people agree as one, it shall be done! (See Matthew 18:19.)

3. Repentance.

Willingness to turn and change the way you think.

> *And so, dear brothers and sisters, I plead with you to give your bodies to God because of all He has done for you. Let them be a living and holy sacrifice—the kind He will find acceptable. This is truly the way to worship Him. Don't copy the behavior and customs of this world, but let God*

transform you into a new person by changing the way you think. Then you will learn to know God's will for you, which is good and pleasing and perfect. Because of the privilege and authority God has given me, I give each of you this warning: Don't think you are better than you really are. Be honest in your evaluation of yourselves, measuring yourselves by the faith God has given us (Romans 12:1-3 NLT).

CHAPTER 13

Getting Started

The following are practical steps that you need to think about and eventually take action on if you are going to start a prayer ministry. Listen to the Holy Spirit speaking to you as you read over these steps. Many thoughts will come to your mind; write them down. Ponder them in your heart and mind over a few weeks to be sure that you are going in the direction God is leading you.

Jesus commanded us to go and share the gospel. Signs should follow us as believers. The first sign was to cast out demons in His name. The last sign listed was to place hands on the sick so they would be healed (see Mark 16:15-18). *This is the Great Commission—not the great suggestion!* Jesus came to destroy the works of the devil (see 1 John 3:8). He also said we would do greater works than He did (see John 14:12).

Prayer Ministry, inner healing, and deliverance are expected ministries of Kingdom believers. Jesus began His ministry quoting from Isaiah 61:1-2:

> *The Spirit of the Lord is upon me, for He has anointed me to bring Good News to the poor. He has sent me to proclaim that captives will be released, that the blind will see, that the oppressed will be set free, and that the time of the Lord's favor has come* (Luke 4:18-19 NLT).

Captives released and the oppressed set free is the Lord's favor! Whom the son sets free is truly free (see John 8:36). I desire to see every church and para-church organization have a prayer ministry team that is trained and equipped to provide healing and deliverance.

First, I would recommend every person experiences a personal time of prayer ministry. This was my experience. I had been a believer for over twenty-five years and I was a pastor when I went to prayer ministry. It was a turning point in my life. Many say, "It was life changing." Our church at Global River offers this ministry and other Bible-believing churches and organizations do as well. Find one so you can experience this step of freedom. Those who seek find, and those who knock see the doors open (see Matt. 7:7).

As the river of God is rising in the earth (see Ezek. 47), the light and the darkness will become more distinct. Our enemy will be exposed and we will have opportunities to minister freedom to others. Let's be ready and equipped. Here are some suggested steps:

- Pray for direction.

- Speak to your church leadership.

- Compile training materials for classroom and practical teachings.

- Provide thorough training and written handouts for trainees.

- Keep records of training.

- Create a spreadsheet of your ministry team that records those who have received ministry training, as well as those who have received prayer ministry.

- Foreign missions—consider this option as these experiences provide a great opportunity to utilize prayer ministry in addition to your church ministry.

- Insurance coverage is paramount—It is vital that you consult your insurance company to see what their criteria are for you or your church. You will most likely need clergy or counselors professional liability coverage.

- Read, study, read, study—Practice

One of my spiritual fathers, Randy Clark, has a Ministry Team Training Manual that I would recommend for equipping. You can also listen to his Breaking Free series of teachings available on audio. Take the opportunity to go on a mission trip with Global Awakening or Global River Church and participate in the deliverance tent and healing tents. Visit his website, www.globalawakening.com, for more information. You will be energized, as the Lord loves people to freedom.

The Destiny Model of Prayer Ministry

*He has delivered us from the power of darkness and con-
veyed us into the kingdom of the Son of His love, in whom
we have redemption through His blood, the forgiveness of
sins* (Colossians 1:13-14 NKJV).

The Destiny Model of Prayer Ministry is the model that my
team has used for healing and deliverance in Africa, South America, Europe, India, Nepal, and the United States. It works well
when the individual is willing to thoroughly let go of his or her
past. Sessions generally take two to five hours. Once a session has
begun, it is best to continue until completion.

Other models allow for "mini" deliverance or prayer to bring
some relief. There is a danger to partial deliverance as the Lord
revealed in Matthew 12:

When an evil spirit leaves a person, it goes in to the desert seeking rest but finding none. Then it says, "I will return to the person I came from." So, it returns and finds its former home empty, swept, and in order. Then the spirit finds seven other spirits more evil than itself, and they all enter the person and live there. And so that person is worse off than before. That will be the experience of this evil generation (Matthew 12:43-45 NLT).

Warning: This ministry is serious and can only be successful if the individual's will is committed to follow Jesus Christ completely and without reservation. Some people are seeking freedom from negative circumstances or bondages, but are actually unwilling to completely renounce the kingdom of darkness. Walking with one foot in the Kingdom of God and one foot in the kingdom of darkness is spiritually dangerous and will open the individual to consequences that are seven times worse (see Matt. 12:43-45).

This ministry is voluntary. The person receiving ministry needs to understand his or her responsibility to prepare for the ministry session and to maintain the freedom after ministry. The person must voluntarily agree to ministry and release the ministry team and those involved from lawsuits or damages.

Prior to performing prayer ministry, a prayer ministry leader should interview every candidate in order to assess the Holy Spirit's leading for deliverance ministry for the individual. Because of the serious nature of deliverance, the following safety precautions should always be employed:

1. People who are heavily medicated should not receive prayer ministry due to the body and soul being unresponsive. *Do not make medical recommendations.* It is never appropriate to

change any medications or treatment; that needs to be left to trained medical providers.

2. Alcoholics and drug addicts should be drug and/or alcohol free for at least two weeks prior to ministry.

3. Deliverance to children less than 18 years of age and pregnant women require specific pastoral approval *prior* to ministry.

4. General prayer can be utilized anytime, whereas prayer ministry that aggressively confronts demonic spirits is done as the Holy Spirit specifically leads. Battle preparations must be made with wisdom and discernment.

5. The individual receiving prayer ministry must:

   • Be a believer in Jesus Christ.

   • Be completely surrendered to the Lord's will.

   • Believe in the gifts of ministry and of the Holy Spirit (see 1 Cor. 12).

   • Be humble and open to full confession of their sins and be willing to forgive others who have brought injury or harm to them. (If the person receiving ministry is not willing to accept these requirements, do not perform prayer ministry.)

6. The ministry team should consist of a team leader, a support-team member, and potentially an intercessor or team member in training. In our church, we require all team members to complete the Global Awakening Ministry Team Training Manual,[1] attend training sessions, read additional required materials, and be released by pastoral leadership for this ministry. It is recommended

that teams are composed of both a man and a woman. *One team member must always be of the same sex as the person receiving ministry.*

7. Select a quiet location that is free from distractions. Be prepared for sessions to last 2-6 hours.

8. No family members are usually present, unless a child is receiving ministry.

Required Team Preparation

1. Complete the Global Awakening Ministry Team Manual.

2. Read *Pigs in the Parlor* by Frank Hammond.

3. Read *Demons and Deliverance* by Frank Hammond.

4. Read *Defeating Dark Angels* by Charles Kraft.

5. Attend training classes if available.

6. Receive prayer ministry for yourself.

7. Be assigned to prayer ministry teams for training.

8. Be released by pastoral or ministry leadership.

Key: This ministry is a ministry of love and freedom; therefore, privacy and confidentiality are foundational to protect the individual's trust of those conducting ministry. Be trustworthy!

Destiny Model Procedures

I. **Covering**

Team:

Submission and Confession.

Prayer (All participants).

Ministry Leader:

Takes authority over all darkness (see Luke 10).

Holy Spirit leading—gifts in operation (see 1 Cor. 12).

Bind spirits of confusion, distraction, distortion, mocking, violence, injury, or harm. Cover team and families under the blood (see James 4:7; Ps. 91; Rev. 12:11).

Confession: Team members and recipient (see 1 John 1:9).

2. **Prayer of salvation and lordship by prayee (best for leader to lead)**

   Test the spirit (see 1 John 4:2-4).

3. **Prayer of total surrender and lifelong commitment to Jesus (prayee)**

   Provide warning regarding reopening doors—consequences are seven times worse (see Matt. 12:43-45).

4. **Prayer of forgiveness (prayee)**

   Choosing to forgive; be specific.

   Prior to prayer:

   • Have prayee share about his or her life, family, and issues/circumstances.

   • Listen in the Spirit for lies and discern spirits in operation.

   • Listen for generational curses, demonic practices, and sin patterns.

A team member should keep notes for prayer to later bind and cast out.

The team leader should ask specific questions about areas of potential sin such as: witchcraft, false religion, sexual sin, bondages, and unforgiveness.

Verbal Prayer by Prayee:

- Forgive all who have caused offenses.

- Renounce curses/bondages.

5. **Prayer of confession of sin (prayee)**

   - Listen in the Spirit for lies and discern spirits in operation.

   - Be prepared for demonic manifestations. Use them to identify areas of focused prayer.

6. **Prayer to break lies of the heart (leader leads)**

   Break soul ties, generational curses, and lies of the heart.

   Note: renouncing curses and breaking lies can also be done during steps 4 and 5 as the Holy Spirit directs.

7. **Prayer of binding and casting out demonic spirits and breaking strongholds (leader, team support)**

8. **Prayer of completion (leader)**

   When the team senses completion by the Holy Spirit, pray for completion and the releasing of all unclean spirits.

   Wait for confirmation from the Holy Spirit.

9. **Prayer of the infilling of the Holy Spirit (prayee—leader helps)**

Pray for the baptism of the Holy Spirit, power, fire (see Luke 11:13; Acts 1:8).

Lay hands on the Prayee and anoint him or her with oil (see Acts 19:1-7; Lev. 8:10-12).

10. **Prayer for release of gifts, fruits of the Spirit (leader or team member)**

    Gifts—1 Corinthians 12.

    Fruits—Galatians 5:22.

11. **Prayer for full armor of God (leader or team member)**

    Ephesians 6:10-18.

12. **Prayer for healing—body, soul, spirit (leader or team member)**

    Father's or Mother's Blessing—prenatal prayer.

    James 5:13-16; anoint with oil.

13. **Prayer to seal and close all unto the Master's hand**

    Hand-cut each other free and give away the file of remembrance. (Protect privacy.)

14. **Give counsel about keeping demonic doors closed and remaining filled with the Holy Spirit**

    - Life of praise and positive words (see Prov. 18:4).

    - Put on the full armor of God (see Eph. 6:10-18).

    - Surrender life daily; guard your thoughts (see 2 Cor. 10:4-5).

    - Stay in the Word and fellowship with believers. Crucify the flesh.

Follow-Up After Prayer Ministry

- Give advice and handouts to the one receiving ministry. (Burn the boats to the old world.)

- Cut the team free—team cleansing.

- Be aware of warfare, of being "slimed." Warriors get dirty. Take time to cleanse and refresh.

- Pray for each other/renew your mind.

- Recommend follow-up ministry.

- Contact for prayer .

- Expect a follow-up attack—this typically happens.

- Identify lifestyle changes that may be needed.

ENDNOTE

1. The Ministry Team Training Manual is available from Global Awakening Ministries. You can order it from their online store: http://globalawakeningstore.com/Ministry-Team-Training-Manual.html.

Prayer of Protection
and Authority

No weapon formed against me will prevail, and I condemn every tongue that rises against me and accuses me. This is my inheritance as a servant of the Lord. My righteousness comes only from You, Jesus. Your blood is more than enough. I apply the blood of Jesus over me, my family, my ministry, and everything that is precious to me. You said you have given us authority over the enemy and that he cannot injure me in any way. I believe Your word in Luke 10:19 where You said that You gave me authority to trample on snakes and scorpions, and that I can overcome all powers of the enemy. Nothing will harm me (Isaiah 54:17, personalized).

You promised blessing in everything I do as I follow Your commands. When the enemy comes against me one way, he will flee seven ways (see Deuteronomy 28:1-7, personalized).

I choose to forgive and bless those who have hurt me or cursed me, but I do not receive their attacks or evil intentions. Because I have submitted to You and Your Word, I resist the enemy and humbly draw close to You, so he must flee in Jesus' name (James 4:7, personalized).

I thank You, Lord, for Your blessings and favor. I resist every instrument or agent from the enemy: sickness, disease, pain, torment, witchcraft, curses, anxiety, fear, doubt, and unbelief. I accept the promised covenant blessings of health, healing, freedom, prosperity, and victory. I choose the overflowing fruit of the Spirit in my life: love, joy, peace, goodness, kindness, gentleness, faithfulness, mercy, and self-control (Galatians 5:22, personalized).

I put on the full armor of God today and submit my life fully to You. Hide me under Your wings so that the enemy can't touch me or my loved ones. Release Your angelic covering (Ephesians 6; Psalm 91, personalized).

With love and devotion to You, my Lord!

Prayer Ministry Preparation Journal

The person receiving prayer ministry should prepare by writing a journal of their preparations, thoughts, and experiences. Bring the journal to the session. It will be destroyed at the end as an act of closure to our past bondages or hurts.

1. Set aside daily prayer and quiet time.

2. Read the following Scriptures and meditate on them:

   • John 10:1-10—Jesus came to give life abundantly.

   • John 14:1-30—The Holy Spirit is given to us to lead us into all truth.

   • First John 1:5-10—Confess your sins for Jesus forgives and cleanses.

   • James 1:5-8—Ask God for wisdom for your freedom.

- James 5:13-18—Confess your sins to each other, so that you may be healed.

- First John 3:1-24—We are *commanded* to love and to forgive.

- Matthew 18:15-35—Choose to forgive and to be forgiven.

3. Prepare private lists of forgiveness and confession.

Please note: it is not uncommon to have several pages for both your Forgiveness List and your Confession List.

Reflect back to your childhood and ask the Holy Spirit to identify those individuals who have created hurts and wounds in your life.

Make another list of your sins to be confessed. Remember to be specific and ask the Holy Spirit to search your heart for anything that is hindering your complete freedom from the past. (If you allow pride or fear to hold back release, you will not be completely freed. It is your choice to let go of the past and to be healed (see James 5:16).)

Note: Ask the Holy Spirit for wisdom and insight along with His divine protection. Remember to bring your journal with you to your prayer session. It will be destroyed after prayer ministry. Your privacy and protection are a vital part of this ministry!

Forgiveness List

Choose to forgive those who have either hurt you or who have created offenses in your life. If you could not stand up in church next to this person and freely worship, then you need to have him or her on your list.

Note: Choosing to forgive does not excuse the sin of others. It simply gives your open wounds to the Lord so He can set *you* free. *This is an act of will, not of your feelings*.

Confession List

Confess all past sins that are revealed to you by the Holy Spirit. This includes thoughts, words, and deeds and encompasses your Christian life as well as your pre-Christian life. Places of guilt and shame are key areas to be explored. Areas to prayerfully explore include:

- False beliefs: false religions, unbelief, idolatry, money, people, false teachings, etc.

- Witchcraft, the occult, New Age: horoscopes, psychics, Harry Potter, Wicca (see Deut. 18:10-14)

- Drugs, alcohol, food, money, hobbies: sin and bondage to any of these

- Sexual immorality: pornography, intimate relationships outside of marriage

- Abuse: verbal, physical, sexual, mental, emotional

- Death music, movies, books: regularly drawn to or exposed to these

- Areas of bondage: repetitive sin that you are trapped in now or have been in the past

- Fears and Anxiety

- Traumatic events: abortion, suicide, violence, deaths, accidents

- Torment or lies: things you know are not true but still struggle with such as rejection, self-hatred or disappointment, doubt of God's love and provision, fear, anger, resentment and hatred, failures

Be aware that prayer ministry is not a "cure all." Please commit to the process before undergoing prayer ministry. The following five actions are recommended after prayer ministry so that you are able to walk in greater levels of freedom and peace:

1. Regularly attend a church or ministry where the Word of God is preached (see Heb. 10:25).

2. Set aside daily time of devotion, prayer, Bible reading, and worship (see Josh. 1:8).

3. Resist sins of action and thought; do not reopen doors where the enemy can gain access. Your will is critical. Remember, resist the enemy and he will flee. Draw close to God, and He will draw close to you (see James 4:7-8).

   So humble yourselves under the mighty power of God, and at the right time He will lift you up in honor. Give all your worries and cares to God, for He cares about you. Stay alert! Watch out for your great enemy, the devil. He prowls around like a roaring lion, looking for someone to devour. Stand firm against him, and be strong in your faith. Remember that your Christian brothers and sisters all over the world are going through the same kind of suffering you are (1 Peter 5:6-9 NLT).

   For we are not fighting against flesh-and-blood enemies, but against evil rulers and authorities of the unseen world, against mighty powers in this dark world, and against evil spirits in the heavenly places (Ephesians 6:12 NLT).

Do not give yourself to any unholy thoughts, sights, sounds, or actions. If you fail, repent, and get back on track.

4. Establish Christian friendships to assist you in walking out your healing. Attend a Bible study or a small group such as a men or women's fellowship.

5. We recommend follow-up prayer ministry. Contact your pastor or ministry team leader for additional prayer about 1-3 months after your first prayer ministry session.

Pre-Ministry Interview Sheet

Prayer Ministry Recipient: _____

Ministry Leader Conducting Pre-interview: _____

_____

Date: _____

Address With Prayee:

1. The individual's reasons for desiring this type of ministry.

2. The purpose of deliverance ministry.

3. The recipient's responsibility prior to counseling session—forgiveness and confession lists to be brought to the session.

4. The risks of the ministry and the necessity of follow-up to maintain freedom.

5. The ministry team approach.

Do you believe the potential Ministry Recipient is a candidate?
_____ Yes _____ No

If no, please explain, use back if needed: _____

_____

_____

_____

Session Date: _____

Ministry Leader _____

Support Member(s) _____

_____

Recipient Release Statement:

I realize this ministry is emotionally and physically draining. I voluntarily submit to this session and will not hold the Ministry Team, or the (List the organization doing the ministry here), or its leadership responsible for any consequences or results. I release them from all recourse:

Signature of Prayer Recipient

_____

Signature of Parent if Recipient is under 18

_____

Date _____

Scriptural Use
of the Word *Sozo*[1]

Salvation

Peter, preaching to the elders and rulers of Jerusalem, said, *"Salvation is found in no one else, for there is no other name under heaven given to men by which we must be saved* [sozo]" (Acts 4:12).

Paul wrote to the Christians at Rome, *"That if you confess with your mouth, 'Jesus is Lord,' and believe in your heart that God raised Him from the dead, you will be saved* [sozo]" (Rom. 10:9).

And to the Church at Ephesus Paul wrote, *"For it is by grace you have been saved* [sozo], *through faith—and this not from yourselves, it is the gift of God..."* (Eph. 2:8).

Healing

Jesus turned and saw her. "Take heart, daughter," he said. "Your faith has healed [sozo] you." And the woman was healed [sozo] from that moment (Matthew 9:22).

And everywhere He went—into villages, towns or countryside—they placed the sick in the marketplaces. They begged Him to let them touch even the edge of His cloak, and all who touched Him were healed [sozo] (Mark 6:56).

"Go," said Jesus, "your faith has healed [sozo] you." Immediately he received his sight and followed Jesus along the road (Mark 10:52).

Deliverance

Those who had seen it told the people how the demon-possessed man had been cured [sozo] (Luke 8:36).

The Lord will rescue [sozo] me from every evil attack and will bring me safely to His heavenly kingdom. To Him be glory for ever and ever. Amen (2 Timothy 4:18).

Though you already know all this, I want to remind you that the Lord delivered [sozo] His people out of Egypt, but later destroyed those who did not believe (Jude 1:5).

Salvation, Healing, and Deliverance!

Jesus said…"For the Son of Man came to seek and to save [sozo] what was lost" (Luke 19:9-10).

Again Jesus said, "Peace be with you! As the Father has sent Me, I am sending you" (John 20:21).

ENDNOTE

1. Randy Clark, *Global Awakening Ministry Team Training Manual* (Pennsylvania: Apostolic Network of Global Awakening, 2011), 25-26.

About Tom Hauser

Tom Hauser is the Senior Pastor of Global River Church, Wilmington, NC. He and His wife Virginia (Ginny) have 4 children and 7 grandchildren. Tom has a Master's degree in Nuclear Engineering and also a Master's in Theology. Prior to his call to ministry, he spent 26 years as an executive for General Electric's nuclear division and motors business. The Lord has used Tom's diversified background, qualifying and training nuclear personnel on the fast attack nuclear submarines, to now war against darkness. Tom teaches and models, *Breaking Free: To Live the Promise of Abundant Life* through prayer ministry for deliverance and inner healing. Randy Clark has "labeled" Tom's team of trained prayer ministers (they run the deliverance tents during Global Crusades around the world) as the Armor Division for Global Awakening missions. The Holy Spirit has inspired the Destiny Model of Prayer Ministry (training manual) as a tool through which the Lord can move deeply in everyone's life. Tom believes he has a mandate from the Holy Spirit to raise up "Samurai" in the spirit for the last days, fueled by purity and passion, and being in the presence of God so that we would be equipped to receive His power and purpose for life and ministry.

PASTOR TOM HAUSER
Address: Global River Church
4702 South College Road
Wilmington, NC 28412
Phone: 910-392-2899 Ext. 2
Email:breakingfree2012@live.com
staff@globalriverchurch.com

In the right hands, This Book will Change Lives!

Most of the people who need this message will not be looking for this book. To change their lives, you need to put a copy of this book in their hands.

> *But others (seeds) fell into good ground, and brought forth fruit, some a hundred-fold, some sixty-fold, some thirty-fold* (Matthew 13:8).

Our ministry is constantly seeking methods to find the good ground, the people who need this anointed message to change their lives. Will you help us reach these people?

> *Remember this—a farmer who plants only a few seeds will get a small crop. But the one who plants generously will get a generous crop* (2 Corinthians 9:6).

EXTEND THIS MINISTRY BY SOWING
3 BOOKS, 5 BOOKS, 10 BOOKS, OR MORE TODAY,
AND BECOME A LIFE CHANGER!

Thank you,

Don Nori Sr., Founder
Destiny Image
Since 1982